14.95

Café

DESIGN

Café
DESIGN

MARTIN M. PEGLER

Visual Reference Publications, Inc. ▪ New York

Visual Reference Publications.
302 Fifth Avenue
New York, NY 10001

Distributors to the trade in the United States and Canada
Watson-Guptill Publishers
1515 Broadway
New York, NY 10036

Distributors outside the United Sates and Canada
HarperCollins International
10 E. 53rd Street
New York, NY 10022

Library of Congress Cataloging in Publication Data:
Café Design
Printed in Hong Kong
ISBN 1–58471–020–9
Designed by Dutton & Sherman

CONTENTS

INTRODUCTION

Dining out today is more than just about food. It is all about food and everything surrounding the food from the color and pattern of the wall coverings, the texture and feel of the flooring underfoot, the tints of the tablecloths and napkins, the style of the china and glassware, the lighting from the overhead chandeliers to the candles flickering on the tabletops. It is about the graphics and artwork on the walls—on the menu—the matchbook cover, and even to the "doggie-bag" that leaves with you. It is about the flowers on the table: a single rose in a bud vase—a spray of small seasonal flowers or some vinyl reproductions set in a pot. Today's dining is about the all-enveloping, all-surrounding "experience." It is the music that is or is not played and if it is played—at what volume. It is about the aromatherapy of mixing the scents of foods, flowers and spices with undertones of expensive perfumes and colognes. It is about artwork, sculpture, antiques, oversized fun figures, hand forged lighting fixtures and scrolled wrought iron railings. It is about the details and the provision of entertainment. It can be "live" entertainment provided by a pianist, a trio or a small combo. It can be a DJ spinning platters, it can be singing waiters or costumed servers or billiard tables and bowling provided to those who would care to partake. It is about how all these details, nuances, subtleties and not so subtle entertainment factors all come together to create a memorable setting for a memorable meal.

Shakespeare would truly find himself in a quandary if he, today, had to answer his own question—"What's in a name?" There was a time when a name meant something and diners knew what was being offered by the name of the establishment. A grill was a grill; a diner a diner; a bar a bar, and a restaurant was a restaurant.

This volume is called Café Design and the "café" in the title does not necessarily refer to a place serving coffee, or to a small, intimate dining space on the Left Bank in Paris. Café is used here as an umbrella term to cover a wide range of informal, casual dining places where the emphasis is on creating a "dining experience." That "experience" can be based on the food, the ambiance, the unique entertainment opportunities, or the mixture of all of the above. These "cafés" are inviting and welcoming and ask only that the diners relax, have fun and enjoy it all. Whether the spaces are highly themed such as Mythos or Rickenbakers, or just touched with foreign elegance such as Abacus, Celadon and Cantaloup, or just warm and wonderful settings for taste sensations such as Bistro Bis, Salute, and Nacional '27, they are all in tune with the millennium and the casual lifestyle that seems to rule supreme.

For this book we have garnered lifestyle cafés from across the USA, Canada, Latin America, Europe and Asia. What makes this edition so international is the universality of the theme: Casual & Informal is in! Here in the U.S. we bring in foreign influences while abroad they interpret some of our American concepts in their own vernacular. It is a small world after all, and the enjoyment of food in attractive and atmospheric surroundings sets that world spinning.

Martin M. Pegler

Café
DESIGN

A N D A L U C A

M A Y F L O W E R   P A R K   H O T E L ,
S E A T T L E ,   W A

Design ▪ Mesher Shing & Associates, Seattle, WA
Robert Mesher/Joe Shing/Cindy Schmidt
Photography ▪ Robert Pisano Photography, Seattle

Located in the Mayflower Park Hotel is the warm and intimate 800 sq.ft. dining space, Andaluca. With a total seating capacity of 70, Andaluca serves meals all day long. The challenge for Mesher Shing, the designers, was to "create an exciting but intimate and sophisticated dining experience" in the limited space.

To achieve their goals the designers/architects utilized two primary design elements. The bar fixture is used both as a focal point for the room and also as a space divider: intimate dining areas are created around it. The high backed dining booths make it possible "to achieve maximum seating capacity and privacy for business lunches and romantic dinners." They also bring rich woods and stylized shapes into the space and all these elements are perfectly accented by the colorful, hand painted mural by Charles Loomis and Irene Ingalls. Charles Loomis also created the whimsical lighting fixtures which "add a lighthearted accent to the upbeat atmosphere where those in casual or formal attire feel equally comfortable."

The soul and spirit of the café's name—Andaluca—appears in the decor, the color and design of the dining area and the artfully designed bar which serves Mediterranean and Northwest U.S. wines. The owners, Birney and Marie Dempcy and the chef, Don Curtis, have produced an "inspired" menu which includes fresh seasonal Northwest foods influenced by the flavors and cooking techniques of the Mediterranean.

Andaluca has won many design awards including the ASID Gold Award for hospitality design and the Gold Key finalist award for excellence in design from Hospitality Design Magazine.

To complement the artistic "fusion cuisine" of chef Kent Rathbun, Engstrom Design Group of San Rafael created Abacus, a 200-seat restaurant/café in Dallas. It is "an exhilarating integration of food, art and architecture." As described by Dotty Griffith, the restaurant critic of the Dallas Morning News, "Abacus is more complex than simple addition, but not as difficult as quantum physics. Compute the elements of a transcendent dining experience: beautifully lit, sensuous decor plus adventuresome, imaginative cuisine multiplied by a delicate balance between formality and fun, and absolutely nothing is left to chance."

What started out as a former billiard parlor on McKinley Ave.—a mixed use neighborhood in urban Dallas—was transformed by the designers at EDG. They added angled geometric planes to the exterior to "provide a sense of depth and interest," and a curved canopy that defines the entrance. Window openings were enlarged and panes of clear and sandblasted glass were inserted to allow views into the space while also providing privacy for the patrons.

ABACUS

DALLAS, TX

Design ▪ Engstrom Design Group, San Rafael, CA
Photography ▪ Richard Klein

"A glistening geometric design motif is adapted in metal and glass throughout the café taking the form of sculpture, custom lighting and metalwork." The interior is filled with bold architectural features which are combined with natural materials, vivid colors and comfortable furnishings. "The design elements create different focal points while reflecting the modern design concept for the restaurant." The space plan starts at the dramatic circular entry and the different dining and bar areas radiate out from it. The open kitchen, in the main dining room, is designed as "an elegant and efficient stage for food preparation." The Chef's Table, directly in front of the kitchen, provides a unique opportunity for special diners to interact with the chef. A smart, semi-private dining room, with direct access to the kitchen, can be screened off for private parties or special occasions. The bar is highlighted by the patterned hardwoods on the floor, the exposed structure and the geometric plastic soffits overhead.

Throughout, abstract works of art are highlighted in Abacus and they add an "Eastern calligraphic feeling" to the space. One series of work is by the noted West Coast artist Jeff Long.

1   Valet Drop-off
2   Entry Vestibule
3   Maitre'd / Host
4   Bar
5   Lounge
6   Dining Room
7   Chef's Table
8   Dining Room
9   Semi-Private Dining Room
10   Men
11   Women
12   Cookline Pick-Up
13   Pantry
14   Kitchen
15   Butcher Shop
16   Prep Kitchen
17   Beverages
18   Chef's Office
19   Dishwash
20   Manager's Office
21   Refrigerator / Freezer
22   Coat Check
23   Wine Storage / Display
24   Waiter Service
25   Valet Station

One of the truly "in" spots for dining on "fusion cuisine" in Sao Paulo is Cantaloup designed by the noted Brazilian architect Arthur de Mattos Casas. In a space that was originally designed for and used as a bakery, Casas has transformed it into a sunny, bright and warm contemporary café. The supporting structure of the roof, which is glass and steel, can fold back electronically to open up the café to the daylight or nighttime breezes. The main facade consists of a pair of large, wood sliding doors.

The space within is divided into two major areas that together can seat 116 guests. The main dining room and bar has a central skylight that floods the space with even more sunshine than already emanates off the happy yellows, golds, and peach tones of the walls, the upholstery and the brilliant artwork on the walls that were painted by Willy Biondani The old brick walls of the bakery have been left exposed but are painted a crisp, bright white as are the corrugated metal panels and trusses that make up the commercial ceiling overhead. The native timber floors have been scraped and then left in their natural color which further enhances the warm analogous color scheme of Cantaloup. The pull-up chairs, designed by the architect, are framed in dark Brazilian "Ipe" and the chairs are upholstered in the sunshine palette of the café design. The chairs at the white, marble topped bar, are slipcovered in the same yellows, golds and oranges. The giant abstract paintings hung on the white-washed walls reiterate the same palette.

The mirror backed wine bar is at one end of the room and its back bar is architecturally framed with pilasters and a cornice above. Throughout, the light is soft, subdued and glowingly reflected off the paintings which are illuminated with spots from above. Wall sconces, at either end of the main room, add to the ambient light. In the second dining room gentle palm trees and other tropical foliage rise up to complement the warm colors and add a touch of atmosphere. When the ceiling is opened, the space is transformed into an open air garden café.

CANTALOUP

SAO PAULO, BRAZIL

Design ▪ Arthur de Mattos Casas, Sao Paulo
Associates ▪ Francisca da Silva/Silvia Carmesini
Photography ▪ Tuca Reines

The Bellagio Hotel/Casino is a must-see sight in Las Vegas. Set in this breathtaking, opulent setting is Sam's American Grill designed by Jordan Mozer & Associates of Chicago. The design firm was responsible for the architecture and interior design as well as the product design and manufacturing services for the Grill.

The entrance from the casino into the casual, 8500 sq.ft. space is delineated by Mozer's signature style in the sculpted columns and railings. The wonderfully amorphous shaped columns support a sinuously curved entablature. Over it, against the black ceiling, are suspended more sculpted forms. The unusual up-lighting fixtures are framed in skeletal forms. According to the designer, the preformed, plaster tree-columns support a grid of twigs that create the ceiling roof. The entry floor is paved with stone. The custom chairs and lighting fixtures plus the rich colors "create a very warm and luxurious room that is modern but comfortable—futuristic but soft and glamorous."

The interior of Sam's American Grill was inspired by the forest and primitive architectural forms "gathered straight from nature." The designer used the imagery of the stripped tree as a column and beam motif throughout.

SAM'S AMERICAN GRILL

BELLAGIO HOTEL/ CASINO, LAS VEGAS, NV

Design ▪ Jordan Mozer & Associates, Chicago, IL
Photography ▪ Doug Snower Photography, Chicago

The floor is richly patterned in dubonnet, celadon, greens, ochers, gold and black. The banquettes and chair backs are upholstered in the same wine color. At one end of the room is the open kitchen which adds a feeling of informality to the space. One long wall is enhanced by a copper "mural" that is varied in color and texture and that picks up many of the colors that appear in the carpet.

According to Jordan Mozer, "We create an alternate reality in our spaces. Our design is the antithesis of rational thought and functionalism. It is based on intuition and emotion". In Sam's American Grill not only does the cuisine set spirits rising but the ambiance prepares the diner for that soaring experience.

CALIFORNIA CAFÉ

SCHAUMBURG, IL

Design ▪ Engstrom Design Group, San Rafael, CA
Consulting Interior Designer ▪ Barbara Hofling
Architect ▪ Hayashida Architects
Photography ▪ Wayne Cable Photography

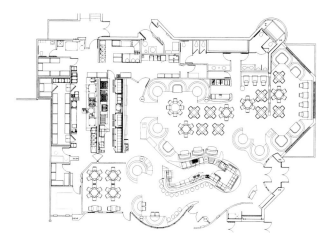

The inspiration for this California Café came not from the state in the name but from nearby Oak Park, IL. The 191-seat space, located in Schaumburg, IL, "takes whimsical inspiration from the architecture of Illinois' native son, Frank Lloyd Wright—and the influence of his Circle Period (1930s and 1940s). As a dining alternative to the "meats & potatoes" menus, this restaurant creates interest and intimacy by directing the diner's view inward and away from the adjacent Woodfield Mall. Playfully interpreted here is Wright's Guggenheim Museum (in N.Y.)—"a curvaceous, almost futuristic, geometry characterizes the restaurant—from the highly visible exterior facade to the interior architecture elements, space plan, furniture, artwork and fixtures."

In the center of the space is the focal, sinuous bar which is adjoined by a semi-circular wine display room. A fluid terrazzo path accesses and encloses the dining room in tones of chartreuse and red while above clusters of circular soffits—finished in vibrant tones of purple, caramel, clay and olive—serve to highlight the dining area below. The circular theme is reinforced by the round and horseshoe shaped booths. Four brilliant copper ring chandeliers serve as icons within the space and are reminiscent of the conical shape of the Guggenheim Museum.

The materials and colors, bold and contemporary, enliven the space. Contributing to the warm, clubby ambiance is the exotic bubinga wood and the stained red cherry millwork. Copper glistens throughout: polished on the aforementioned chandeliers, hammered and used to cover structural columns and acid washed to form the hood over the open kitchen. In the main dining room, the cookline "enters into a dynamic visual interplay with the colorful cracked linen mural that encloses the area."

California artisans created many of the custom art pieces like the forged iron and blown glass light fixtures, the reflective art glass dividers, the '50s inspired, torn page collages and the copper features. "Great food in a playful, elegant environment is a concept that works at California Café."

T J K CAFÉ

L I T T L E N E C K , N Y

Design ▪ Eric Song, Owner
Photography ▪ Sam Kim

he space is small—very small—only 1440 sq.ft. and it is long and narrow. Located in a "neighborhood" just outside of NYC, the owner/designer, Eric Song, wanted to create a contemporary look with a feeling of spaciousness and warmth and yet keep the costs down. "We wanted to create a casual, upbeat atmosphere where customers could feel at home and we don't want to alienate anyone." Since most of the "regular" diners are repeat customers, the main objective was to draw a new and expanded clientele. The original interior was demolished and in the new, open space the owner/designer managed space for a full service restaurant as well as a casual wine/beer bar. By closing off the kitchen Song was able to save on heating and cooling as well as minimizing the noise and odors that emanate from a busy kitchen. It was also important not only to maximize the seating but to make the seating comfortable and in a noise-free zone. The seating also had to be flexible to accommodate intimate dining as well as larger groups or private parties in the limited space.

The design palette consists of a mixture of woods (oak, birch and maple) some of which were stained cherry red or deep blue. The reddish color dominates on the wainscoting and around the back bar up front near the entrance. The walls were texture painted to simulate a celadon green suede fabric and the floor is paved with earth tone ceramic tiles. A slightly off-center aisle leads diners from the bar to the rear. One long perimeter wall is taken up with a long bench that has been softened with loose pillows of red and blue while loose angled tables and chairs fill in the opposite side of the aisle. MR 16 lamps were used for a "softer effect" while during the daylight hours sunlight filters through the glazed facade of T J K's Café. Swoops of red and navy fabric, on the light colored ceiling, break down the length of the room into smaller, more intimate components.

SONOMA

CHARLOTTE, NC

Design ▪ Shook Design Group, Charlotte, NC
Principal in Charge ▪ Kevin Ervin Kelley, AIA
Architect ▪ Frank Quattrochi
Interior Design ▪ Cicely Worrell
Photography ▪ Tim Buchman

The designers of Sonoma, a new café/restaurant/bar in Charlotte, NC were inspired by the California wine country for the name for their design concept. Though it is located in a 14-story business building, Sonoma suggests a relaxed casual ambience through its warm, earthy colors, hand wrought materials and the sunlit, open spaces.

Shook Design Group created two separate moods: a passive, softer space for dining and a more active space with a dynamic presence for cocktails and appetizers. Though situated on a highly trafficked street, there is a wrap-around outdoor patio that can accommodate 50 patrons. There is indoor seating for just under 140. Glass walls on the street corner tend to bring the street into the restaurant. "By placing most of the color and active wall planes at the back edge of the space, the interior design visually draws attention through the restaurant."

The wine room is placed up front to encourage the wine sales and also to set the theme. A focal element in this area is the Cruvient Tap System which allows Sonoma to offer and dispense over 80 wines by the glass. There are more than 350 wines to choose from and thus, not surprisingly, more than half the receipts are from wine sales.

In the dining room small, intimate pockets of seating were created through the use of alcoves, corners, curtained zones and ceiling definitions "that seem to float in the night sky." The walls are faux textured in ocher, butterscotch, terra cotta and ultramarine. The break up of the applied colors also tends to break up the large space into smaller, more select seating areas. A herringbone pattern of plum and beige carpet tiles zig-zags across the floor and the bar area is defined by the rustic slate tile flooring. "The use of contrasting materials such as the glass and metal storefront with the natural wood millwork of the back bar help to balance urban austerity with comfortable elegance."

OPEN CORK

TORONTO, CANADA

Design ▪ Hirschberg Design Group, Toronto
Photography ▪ Richard Johnson, Interior Images

Though located in Toronto, Open Cork, as designed by the Hirschberg Design Group, takes its inspiration from the naughty days of old New Orleans. The rustic look of the previous tenant was banished and mostly replaced by linear and bold elements.

The New Orleans theme is expressed in the brothel-style, high back, round settee sitting out in the center of the dining room. It is upholstered in a florid, flamboyant pattern of palm fronds on a dark green background. Growing out of the top of the circular seating unit is a stylized palm tree. The walls are finished in an icy cool, cucumber green which contrasts with the deep, dark woods and the rich wine-red carpet. A striped fabric that combines the greens and reds and also a frenzied foliage print are used to upholster the booth seating and the banquettes.

In the bar area the colors are warmer and the ash veneer bar is stained a dark brown walnut color. The red orange color appears on the wood floor. The bar top is zinc plated steel and galvanized steel furniture and fittings accentuate the color scheme. The rattan fans whirring overhead further the New Orleans inspiration.

The white textured ceiling and the antique, white-rubbed wood contrast with the deep burgundy color in the glass walled wine making room. The corrugated ceiling and the rustic wood details are remnants of the previous owner's interior design. The glass beaded curtain—another New Orleans touch—serves as a separator of the moderne but warm dining room from the bar which is even warmer in appearance and in color.

BEN'S KOSHER DELI

〜〜〜〜〜〜〜〜〜〜〜〜〜

NEW YORK, NY

Design ▪ Haverson Architecture & Design, Greenwich, CT
Design Team ▪ Jay Haverson/Carolyn Haverson/Michael Kaufman/Lisa Bianco/Gina Librandi/Nick Lios
Photography ▪ Paul Warchol Photography

Kosher dining is to some what haute cuisine might be to others. It is for a "specialized taste" that for some may be acquired but to others it is what comes after mother's milk. For decades—back to the 1920s—Lou G. Siegel's old-fashioned, dark wood paneled restaurant was the mecca for diners looking for a "strictly kosher dining experience." Replacing it now is Ben's Kosher Deli: a new, bright, fresh setting for a new, light, more diverse Kosher menu. The 225-seat space, as designed by Haverson Architecture & Design of Greenwich, CT exudes a warm, welcoming and playful atmosphere in which one can enjoy a pastrami sandwich that is a meal in itself or lighter kosher delights.

The prominently-lit canopy that extends out across the entire front of the restaurant proclaims, "We cure our own corned beef. Our chicken soup cures everything else." There is humor—Yiddish style—throughout the design. It starts on the street and brings them in laughing. Incorporated into the signage is an overscaled clock. It symbolizes "continuity" while also admitting to the rebirth of modern Kosher cooking. The extensive use of glass on the facade permits the passing public to view the tempting deli operation on one side and the bar and main dining room on the other. The Deli runs the full length of the west wall and opens—seamlessly—to the main dining room on the opposite side. Though the space is still long and narrow, it appears somewhat more square due to the skillful use of a folding partition wall. It delineates the two private dining rooms at the rear.

"Characteristic of the culture, a lightheartedly poking fun at one's self prevails in the humorous, slice of life Yiddish jokes" that are hand stenciled in gold in bands along the wall. A Chagall inspired ceiling mural—also banded with Yiddish jokes—highlights the dining room setting. The mural is alive with floating, dream-like figures that represent everyday life in the NY Garment and Theater districts, the "old country" and Jewish culture and traditions. Mixed in are icons of the past like Eddie Cantor and symbols of the present: the Empire State building. Backlit with warm fluorescents, the mural is a softly draped series of panels that run between the beams.

The terrazzo floor is patterned with images of foods and "familiar heart-warming objects." The decoratively faux painted walls and soffits suggest the parchment on which the Torah is written. "The antique texture and warm amber hue softly lend balance to the light and dark woods that alternate throughout the space." Bow backed ban-

quettes and booths are upholstered in a chevron patterned fabric of grape, cranberry, and mango. The "food" colors are also echoed in the multi-colored glass throughout and in the mural above.

Combine all this with the music of violins, the uncorked wine bottle waiting up front, the taste of pickles at the deli counter, and Ben's appeals to all the senses—especially a sense of humor. Ben's Kosher Deli "speaks to living life to the fullest, an abundance of lively conversations with friends while feasting on the Kosher fare of one's choice in the comfort of familiar, visually rich surroundings." L"Chaim !!

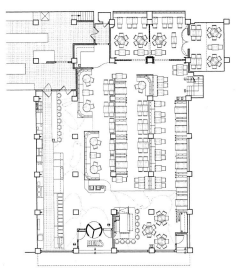

CANADIAN BAR & GRILL

TORONTO, CANADA

Design ▪ Hirschberg Design Group, Toronto
Photography ▪ Richard Johnson, Interior Images

Creating a "Canadian" setting for a restaurant that features Canadian specialties fell to the Toronto based design firm, Hirschberg Design Group. Armed with Canadian details and motifs and inspired by the natural landscapes of the country, the designers converted the existing restaurant space off a hotel lobby into a new dining experience. This was all accomplished within a tight time frame and a constrictive budget.

All the millwork, existing or new, was refinished into a two tone cherrywood finish—for "a monochromatic effect." The slate tile floor finish was extended into the hotel's lobby "to create a patio feel without a major change of architecture." The existing risers were modified and now successfully

define one area of the restaurant from another. To affect a
unique but truly Canadian ambiance the designers specified
frosted crackle glass to "illustrate" the Northern lakes, birch
tree branches and natural stonework on some feature walls.
"For this project artifacting was the key: the use of natural
materials, artifacts, and memorabilia such as a river rock wall
mural, canoes, snow shoes, and other typically 'Canadian'
symbols." These all together help to create the sort of "silent
entertainment" that goes with the specific menu.

The buffet area in the atrium is furnished with street facing
windows. These allow the sunshine to filter in during the
daylight hours—"creating a warm and airy environment."

McGRATH'S FISH HOUSE

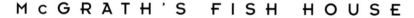

BOISE, ID

Design ▪ G. S. Beckham Design Associates, Costa Mesas, CA

Photography ▪ Milroy & McAleer

The design concept was to make the space feel as though it had once been a fishing cannery—long abandoned—and now coming back into use. Thus, the old brick facade and the wealth of weathered and aged graphics. McGrath Fish House, in Boise, ID, is part of an eight unit chain and this design was to be "a new approach to bringing the chain to a new level of sophistication" while also providing the perfect background for the extensive fresh seafood menu. The restaurant was to be a "visually exciting environment that displays historical references to the Pacific Northwest fishing heritage."

G. S. Beckham Design Associates of Costa Mesa, CA made special use of the Oyster Bar by placing it up front for its visual display power and service function. It is situated in view of the entry and it is also critically located within the guest flow. Casual sidewalk seating for the Oyster Bar is within the Gallery Monitor—"thus turning a circulation corridor into a seating area that provides a terrific view of all activities of the facility."

There are three dining rooms and each has its own distinctive flavor. The largest has the used brick "old cannery" wall as a backdrop along with mahogany tables and booths to create a warm and inviting old-fashioned environment. The second dining room can accommodate large groups due to the creative booth placement but still make guests feel individual and comfortable. The "Library Cove" is the smallest of the three areas and it resembles a ship captains' library. It is finished with a high wainscot of

mahogany. The Bar blends the rustic personality of hand carved totem poles, punched tin panels and pine end-block with the traditional beauty of stained mahogany and art nouveau "cat-tail" torcheres. Hard surface, multi-colored quartzite flooring provides a rough hewn texture yet it is easily maintained. "The rugged nature of the natural stone contrasts beautifully with the mahogany and polished granite surfaces nearby."

The concept of blending rustic and polished materials is evident throughout the Fish House and suggests "a transformation of space rather than a static background." "Visual activity and action therefore contribute to and complement the experience, rather than becoming a distraction." Throughout McGrath's there is a creative mix of local historical black and white photos as well as mounted fresh water fish, antiques, artifacts, and memorabilia that all add up to the look of the restaurant and enhance the dining experience.

The transformation of an existing restaurant into an exciting dining experience called Jack Mackerel's Island Seafood is the work of the Shook Design Group of Charlotte, NC. "The concept was to take the patron away from the 'everyday' with a sense of adventure, romance, and casual fun in food, service and atmosphere." The result is this 6400 sq. ft. seafood house and Barracuda Bar with a slightly upscale, dinner only, grill with 180 seats and a bar/patio/deck that can accommodate another 64 patrons.

The exterior was given an architectural "facelift" and now resembles a Key West Victorian mansion. The towers with interior illumination were added and the cornice was rebuilt and accented with light sconces. The existing metal roof, now aquamarine blue, sits atop the tropical white building. Adding to the Key West ambiance are the Bahamian gazebo, a fountain, the deck and the "reef runner" mural—all dramatically washed with light. All together they add up to a lovely night time place to be.

The interior is open and inviting. The original space was gutted and dark stained timber has been sandblasted. The bar was extended and is now capped with an illuminated wood canopy of bottles and tropical glasses. A "rustic" eight foot barracuda—like an old weathered tropical sign—sits over the bar and signals the entry. The big challenge was to maintain "a touch of class" in what could easily be a tacky tropical wannabe. Instead, a festive setting was created with Turkish market lanterns on sailboat cables, and dramatic

JACK MACKEREL'S ISLAND SEAFOOD

CHARLOTTE, NC

Design ▪ Shook Design Group, Charlotte, NC
Principal in Charge ▪ Kevin Ervin Kelley, AIA
Project Architect/Designer ▪ Michael Nicholls, AIA
Interior Design ▪ Cicely Worrell: Interior Design
Communications Designer ▪ Ginger Reilly
Graphics Designer ▪ Jeff Camillo
Architect ▪ Vince Ciccarelli, AIA
Graphic Designer ▪ Wendi Ferguson
Architects ▪ Tracy Finch/Kevin Kennedy/Frank Quattrochi
Photography ▪ Tim Buchman

lighting effects through the bamboo canopies that help to camouflage the HVAC systems overhead. They also add a sense of dining intimacy without detracting from the openness of the space. Custom lamps and sconces of grass cloth are used atop the Key West style interior railings. Bamboo is used in myriad and often unexpected ways: fishing pole style masts, floating canopies, bar die panels, wall caps and even as door handles for the bathrooms.

In addition, the interior is rich in Caribbean murals and folk artwork. There are tropical plants reproduced in silk that appear in urns and casks. The maps and antique nautical charts that decorate the Barracuda Bar also are reproduced on the menu cover. Jack Mackerel's evokes a sense of adventure and fun in a casual ambiance that appeals to "the vacation deprived Boomer audience" by providing a dining-out/travel experience close to home.

DANTE'S SEAFOOD GRILL

PIER 39, SAN FRANCISCO, CA

Design ▪ Ohashi Design Studio, Oakland, CA,
Alan Ohashi & Joy Ohashi
Photography ▪ John Sutton Architectural Photography

ante's is a popular sea food restaurant on the very heavily trafficked Pier 39 in the San Francisco Bay area. Tourists flock here for the view, the sights, the shopping and the fresh seafood. The original Dante's 6500 sq. ft. restaurant is on the upper level of the two level pier and was missing the exposure to the more heavily visited lower level. When a space became available directly below, the owners called upon Alan and Joy Ohashi of Ohashi Design Studio in nearby Oakland to turn the 700 sq. ft. space into a café/bar.

The new café/bar is visually linked to the restaurant upstairs by an opening in the floor which gives guests below an opportunity to "sample" what awaits above. A glass elevator brings diners up from below and a dumbwaiter brings the prepared foods down from the kitchen upstairs to be served to the patrons in the café. The designers used a combination of cool colors: a celadon green and a washed down marine blue on the walls . These are complemented by the warm cherry wood flooring, bar and seating. The chairs and bar stools are upholstered in green and blue and bright red pendant lights punctuate the space. In addition, the designers created the 1000 sq. ft. outdoor dining area with a tempered glass windscreen that allows diners to enjoy the

view of San Francisco Bay and the adjacent marinas.
Between the deck and the café another 50 guests can be
served in addition to the 300 that can be accommodated
in the restaurant upstairs.

Amid the visual excitement of beckoning signage in
this tourist center, the Ohashi's added facade signage
"that reflects the renewed spirit and ambiance of the
restaurant."

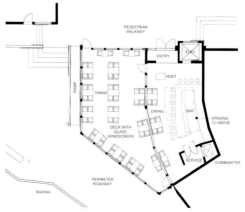

THE FISH HOUSE

TORONTO, CANADA

Design ▪ Hirschberg Design Group, Toronto
Photography ▪ Richard Johnson, Interior Images

Hirschberg Design Group of Toronto was invited to oversee the renovation of an existing restaurant/bar space into a café that would seem as fresh as the "catch of the day" that appeared on the menu. The 242-seat seafood restaurant occupies 4000 sq. ft. and an additional space of 1680 sq. ft. is home to The Shucker's Bar. Within a tight budget and a limited time span, the designers needed to completely change the exterior and interior look of The Fish House into a bright, fresh seafood lover's haven.

The design firm established a nautical theme within a crisp, contemporary architectural statement. Custom, fish shaped light fixtures "swim" throughout the neutral beige interior. Textured beaded glass panels are framed by "weather washed and sun bleached" wood beaded board panels while below the planked timber floors carry through the same look. Criss-crossing over the off-white, textured ceiling are assorted lengths of "floating" timber stained a deep brown color. Schools of cut out, metal abstract fish shapes swim across the textured glass panels and an occasional "fish" floats sideways and serves as a

shield for a single lamp bulb. Adding to the textural context is the rough stone wall that frames the blackboard which features the chalked on specials of the day.

Several swirling, wave-like banquettes add to the flow of the space and they are upholstered in an abstract print of many subdued colors. The seats are covered in blue. The pull up chairs are dark brown wood and the white undercloths are topped with wrapping paper squares to carry through the beige palette. To create a sense of warmth and also a feeling of an old inn, somewhere near the sea, the fireplace in the main dining room is flanked by cubicles filled with wine bottles and a painting of an ancient mariner hangs over the mantle. Several trophy fish arc and jump across the walls and they are highlighted by spots sheltered amid the timbers suspended from the ceiling.

MOISHES

~~~~~~

TORONTO, CANADA

Design ▪ ll X lV Design Associates, Toronto
Photography ▪ David Whittaker

The new, enlarged and greatly upscaled Moishes is now located in a two-level, 10,000 sq. ft. space in the First Canadian Place bank tower. II X lV Design Associates of Toronto undertook the design of this new restaurant for the sons of the original founder who established Moishes in 1938. Unlike the usual heavy and overwhelmingly masculine approach to steak houses, the owners and designers agreed upon a lighter and more flamboyant vision: one more in keeping with today's consumer lifestyles.

It starts out front where II X IV added a highly visible street entrance with a huge "storefront" window that provides views of both floors. The lobby which serves both the street and mall entrances has herringbone brick veneer arched ceilings uplit by fixtures concealed behind canted side walls. These walls are faced with woven Spanish cedar. Moishes logo, in tinted concrete and zinc, is inlaid in the ashlar patterned limestone floor. A sensuously sculpted wine cabinet displays a selection of wines and liquors while it also serves as a backdrop for the waiting area seating. In the main floor casual dining lounge, the banquette seating is supplemented with club chairs, sofas and cocktail tables. The overscaled scrolled ends of the banquettes recall the wine cabinet up front. The rich, lush upholstery fabrics are detailed with diamond tufted backs and bolsters. Beyond the sandblasted glass and olive ash burl panels is the private cognac/cigar lounge which is quieter and somewhat more formal. Humidors are stored in the "doors and drawers" paneling along one wall and the wood that surmounts the green onyx faced fireplace repeats the previously mentioned scroll motif. Seating is in clusters around the inset area rugs. The wing back chairs are covered in a bitter chocolate tufted chenille fabric.

The ceiling below the mezzanine area is very low so light finishes were used in this area. A traditionally patterned stenciled wall is finished in cream on cream and it complements the walnut stained, olive ash burl and mappa burl woods. The building's Edwardian white marble cladding has been retained on the integral columns and wall faces so the designers used the same marble to top bars, vanities and console tables. Other columns are wrapped in exaggerated wooden curves. A new staircase was installed to connect the two levels and wine cabinets and coat check areas are tucked in under the stairs. At the top is an exquisitely detailed bar built around a large column. Built-in cabinets, behind, display bottles of wine.

The seating for 250 diners includes the two small private dining rooms recessed behind pocket doors. In the large main dining room, floating ribbons of dry wall, outlined in light, break up the vast ceiling space and also reduce sound reflection. The extra high chair backs not only divide the space into quieter and more intimate groupings but also give diners a feeling of privacy. In the smaller rooms the light fixtures are recessed in the burl wood ceiling panels.

"Moishes Toronto is sophisticated but comfortable. It looks back to its heritage but presents the new face of steak houses today."

F O R K

PHILADELPHIA, PA

Design ▪ Marguerite Rodgers Ltd., Philadelphia, PA
Photography ▪ Matt Wargo Photography

Located in the old historic section of Philadelphia, Fork is an "American Bistro" set in a rehabilitated shell of an historically certified building on Market St. With 15 ft. ceilings, exposed duct work and natural cast iron columns, the space has a sense of history.

Marguerite Rodgers was called upon by Ellen Yin, a co-owner of Fork, to create a restaurant which would reflect the area's long history as an artists' community and also serve as the setting for the creative cuisine that features fresh seasonal products at reasonable prices. Rodgers' transformation of the space called upon the talents of the area's top artisans.

The walls are now texturally painted in soothing shades of green, blue and ocher and the long windows are framed with velvet drapes rich in geometric patterns and symbols. Totally impressive are the giant light fixtures with their hand painted shades that hang down from the high ceiling. The black lacquered columns serve as dramatic exclamation points in the setting. Featured in the 48-seat dining room are seven ft. high banquettes along the perimeter wall with taupe/gray upholstered chairs and divider partitions. The wheat gold tablecloths echo the glowing warmth of the ocher textured walls above the

gray stained wood wainscot. The 30-seat lounge offers "a social setting" with small charcoal sofas and a unique, cast concrete bar. Weather permitting, there is a small sidewalk café that can accommodate ten guests.

Up front, at the entrance, guests are treated to an antique mosaic "doormat" with forks as the dominant decorative motif that sets the scene for the restaurant that follows. With the building's Old City character, the creative artwork and unique furniture, Fork is a very "visual" restaurant and the open kitchen is a source of wonderful entertainment that regales the senses. USA Today wrote: "Every neighborhood needs an affordable, stylish bistro like Fork."

B O B A

T O R O N T O ,   C A N A D A

Design ▪ II X IV Design Associates, Toronto
Photography ▪ David Whittaker

The noted Toronto design firm, II X IV Design Associates, was challenged by Bob Bermann and Barbara Gordon to "create a sense of attachment for place" in the somewhat, out-of-the-way, old brick house in which three previous fine restaurants had failed. The new design would have to be "startling in its simplicity yet gracefully support the extraordinary skills" of the chef and the cuisine to be offered.

According to the designers, "The colors, shapes and savory smells of the food itself were to play key roles, within an airy, serene backdrop for conversation, laughter and delicious eating." The redesign started with the exterior where the roof trim, window frames and shutters were painted burgundy and blue to set off the gold brick facing of the building. A lush, provincial garden was created out front, contained within a wrought iron fence.. Baskets and planters overflow with flowers and vines and a huge, gold and navy awning provides shade from the sun for the out-of-doors diners.

Inside the small restaurant which is filled with intimate spaces, the provincial feeling continues. The many beautiful, vibrant colored floral paintings are from the owners own collection. They not only adorn the walls but they provide the color palette of lavender, gold, green and blue. These colors are applied to the walls and the floors combine earth tones and neutral brickwork. All together, they provide a "garden like setting" for the warm maple tones of cabinetry, chair frames and table legs. A feminine softness is infused into the design through the use of elegant, sinuous curves in the woodworking. To create a more open atmosphere and yet not lose the intimacy and charm inherent in the old building, the walls between the smaller, low-ceilinged spaces were partially demolished and thus affected open views from one area into the next.

The dining rooms on the main level are more intimate in scale than the large dining room on the second level which has an exposed roof structure. The ceiling was painted white "to exaggerate its height and reflect more light—flooding the attic with sunlight." In addition to the colorful artwork, the white tablecloths are set with colorful plates and bright hued vases are filled with fresh flowers. According to a review in Toronto Life, "There's no room for outlandish, designer-driven impracticalities in the simple, prettily painted space. Colorful canvases and tasseled lampshades are more cheerful than mysterious."

BISTRO BIS

15TH ST. S.W., WASHINGTON, DC

Architect/Design ▪ Adamstein & Demetriou
Architects, Washington, DC
Principals in Charge ▪ Olvia Demetriou &
Theodore Adamstein
Project Architect ▪ Lance Hosey
Interior Design ▪ Michaela Robinson
Project Team ▪ Joel Mendelson
Photography ▪ Theodore Adamstein

Chef Jeff Buben, and his wife Sallie, the owners, knew exactly what they wanted when they called in Adamstein & Demetriou to create their new dining space in Washington DC. According to the architects/designers, "We were asked to provide a design that would capture the spirit of a Paris bistro—drawing on the traditional, evocative imagery but with an innovative and contemporary approach." The design had to be visually exciting, yet warm and inviting and provide for an energized but comfortable dining experience. The challenge was mainly the space: a concrete shell broken into disjointed parts and there was a front atrium with a three sided mezzanine, a small central room with a low ceiling and a two story back wall. The designers had to "dramatize this configuration" into as series of interconnected spaces.

Relying on familiar classic French bistros, brasseries and cafes, Adamstein & Demetriou joined the varied dining experiences along an axial spine. Upon entering, the diner focuses on the length of the circulation of the spine towards an enticing view of the rotisserie and kitchen. "A feeling of transparency and openness runs through the restaurant, from front to back, allowing diners in all areas to feel connected to the action."

The front space is home to the double height bar which is enhanced by the two story fenestration to the street and the outdoor dining patio. A "smoking lounge" on the mezzanine overlooks the focal bar which is highlighted by a 12-ft. high mirror, backlit glass panels and bottle display. A string of table lamps, along the bar top, provide a feeling of warmth. Taking advantage of the low ceiling in the

central area, the designers made this the cozier and more intimate dining area with deep booth seating. It is still connected to other parts of the bistro with views to the other spaces. The circulation corridor was angled to affect an experience-filled path from the entrance to the dining rooms and then ending at the open kitchen.

Warm neutral materials such as cherry and maple wood panels play up against surfaces of stainless steel, glowing etched glass louvers and the stainless and coated steel ornamental ironwork. The traditional bistro mosaic floor has been "reinterpreted" with large zig-zag tiles. The tear

drop shaped pendants that hang in the dining hall are a variation on the classic bistro globe light. The custom made chandeliers are reminiscent of the over-scaled paper lamp shades and the specially made steel, roll-edged bar emulates the zinc bars found in French cafes and bistros. A two story column is covered with a mural by Lemore Winters Studio which is done in the style of French painters in the 1920s..

"The result is a restaurant that is bold and sensual in design but has the warmth and simplicity of a classic eatery."

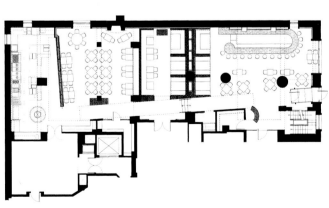

ROUGE 98

PHILADELPHIA, PA

Design ▪ Marguerite Rodgers Ltd., Philadelphia
Photography ▪ Matt Wargo Photography

eil Stein, a visionary restaurateur, knew exactly what he wanted when he commissioned Marguerite Rodgers to create Rouge 98. This was to be a restaurant/bar/outdoor café that people of all ages could enjoy and relate to. He wanted "a lively European Bistro atmosphere."

Marguerite Rodgers' inspiration for this relaxed café/bistro/lounge was a 1920's French parlour. The intimate, 50-seat restaurant is a "stage set" with warm brown textured velvet settees, chairs upholstered and decorated with cording and bullion fringe and walls draped from ceiling to floor with a shimmering, pale dusty pink fabric. There is also in the design an acknowledgment of "La Belle Epoque"—that opulent period in France when the nineteenth century was ending. It was a period when fashion, art, culture and night-life flourished and was inspired by the work of painter/socialite Florine Stetheimer, the architect/designer Eliel Saarinen and the sculptor Constantin Brancusi. "Now that we have reached the turn of the twentieth century, La Belle Epoque has returned with all its glamour and romanticism," says Miss Rodgers.

To give the diners the feeling that they are in the "bois" or in the park, Rouge 98 which is located on the park-like and fashionable Rittenhouse Square in central Philadelphia, the designer provided tall, elegant French doors that can be opened up—weather permitting. The small, 18-seat outdoor café actually allows the fortunate few to dine "al fresco" in the park.

Throughout the interior space there are elegant touches such as the Gustav Klimt-inspired hand painted verre eglomise mirrors, the ornate wall sconces and the framed mirrors. A focal point—other than the park outside—is the unusual bi-level oval bar in the center of the restaurant. The white top with its scalloped edges sits over a sculpted bronze base. A radiating pattern of carpet panels accentuates the bar's location. The balance of the floor is carpeted in a deep wine red. Mahogany trim, panels and frames also add to the overall sophisticated look of Rouge 98.

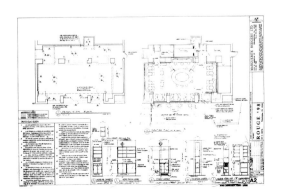

CAFFÉ DEGLI ARTISTI

ROME, ITALY

Design ■ Studio Ciccotti, Rome

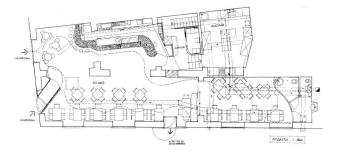

Much of the popularity and the sense of intimacy that has been achieved in the design of the Caffe Degli Artisti—a Bohemian café in Rome—was the result of a serious structural problem. The architects/designers, Studio Ciccotti, had to reduce the stress on the internal load bearing walls. To achieve this they removed the layers of plaster that had been applied over the years only to reveal "the aesthetic beauty of the old brick and tuff primitive walls." To reinforce the walls, the iron trusses that were used created crisp decorative black outlines throughout. To balance the "weightiness" of the brick and stone, the designers emphasized the lightness in the balance of the palette. According to the designers, "This balance became the leitmotif concept" with light colors on the ceiling, in the colors and forms of the fittings and furniture, the lighting plan, and even the "glistening reflections of the steel on the bar counter." The HVAC systems which snake through this bi-level café is also light, bright and reflectively shiny.

The dynamic young owners/ managers of the café wanted to recapture the essence of the "artiste's" cafes of Paris in the 1960s and 1970s when live entertainment, often impromptu, was part of the action. In order to accommodate this "show space," Studio Ciccotti left open areas with "free walls" and introduced a lighting system that is flexible and easily adaptable to highlighting a live performance.

In contrast to the rough texture of the walls, the floor is treated industrial cement. One of the "lightening" efforts is visible in the maple wood bar that has been washed down with white. A wave pattern of brushed steel serves as the base beneath the wood. Off-white molded plastic chairs with spindly chrome legs complement the tall, backless bar stools. The major accent color—other than the black outlining trusses—is the Pompeian rose/red color that accentuates some of the new plaster jambs around doors and also used on the ceiling of the mezzanine extension of the café.

This café appeals to an audience of 25- to 40-year olds and the fare consists mainly of pizzas, baguettes, beverages—and good music.

CARROT'S CAFÉ

~~~~~~~~~~~~~~~

ROME, ITALY

Design ▪ Studio Ciccotti, Rome

arrot's Café is, according to its designers, meant to appeal to an audience of 20 to 40 year olds who are into the club/pub/café scene. The Roman design firm, Studio Ciccotti, has approached the project in a non-traditional manner since they feel that their targeted audience is also non-traditional and non-conformist.

The small space is filled with assorted high tech/industrial textures from the rough faced brick laid both vertically and horizontally to the embossed sheets of stainless steel used to face the bar to the chains that link the legs of the custom bar stools. In trying to emulate the warmth and comfort of an old wine cellar—but updated—Studio Ciccotti combined wood and brick which are ties to the past with steel which represents the new and the innovative.

Concrete floors are painted and the walls are stained with rich, clashing colors and the colored lights play havoc with the colors and the textures. There is nothing that is "quaint and charming" here nor is there meant to be. As the designers explain, the Italian trend is towards new and way out spaces and not the old fashioned English style pubs. "Italians don't prefer to drink beer and they prefer a place that is fun and continuously enjoyable. The guest's priorities are to drink and eat something special in a place where one can socialize: meet friends, listen to music— good music—in a scenographic sphere."

PIANTA DEGLI ARREDI

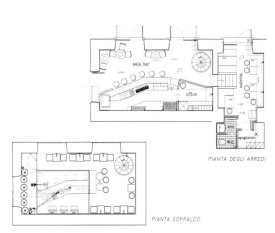

PIANTA SOPPALCO

Carrot's offers an original space with a distinctive look and ambiance. The small bar yields to a variety of seating options. There are booths upholstered in red, red-violet, and blue vinyls with ground steel bases accented with chains. The free standing, burner-like stools are also made of the patterned metal and are trimmed with the chains. The bar and some of the seating is at ground level and a few steps down—below grade level—is Carrot's Room: a small, cellar-like and very intimate space. A spiraling staircase with perforated metal treads leads to the upper storage mezzanine that surrounds the bar. The ceiling is filled with HVAC systems, pipes, ducts and beams—all painted with the same "stained" wash as the walls. Drop lights, at assorted heights, add to the warm, rich ambient glow of the space.

ove off the Pacific Highway at Laguna Beach, avoid the bustle, and step into the romance and charm of a turn-of-the-century (19th into 20th) Paris Café/Bistro. Though set inside an unassuming cottage, Hatch Design Group of Costa Mesa has magically transformed the space. "The feel is a touch of nostalgia brought back, dusted off and given a new paint and a new attitude."

The small Tudor-style cottage was built in 1938 and is filled with small rooms. The designers, having researched French styles and colors of the 1930s and 1940s, have furnished the various dining rooms with custom, scaled down furniture to create a series of delightful settings. Inspired by the "organic, curving, sinewy shapes and forms" found in art deco art and design. The result is expressed in bowed booths, radiused settee backs and the "animated life-like forms" of the dining room chairs. Texture and color are used to affect mood and attitude and the designers have specified dark aneigre wainscoting, vertical channeled leather booths and plush mohair upholstered dining chairs.

The "scenario" was to create an overall "romantic" setting and thus, each of the four dining rooms is done in a special color with a seating style of its own. The seating can vary from chairs to banquettes to booths trimmed with hobnail studs. Fires burn in the two hearths and black and white photos abound on the walls. According to Jeff Hatch, the designer, "There is nothing grand about French 75 but the restaurant is rich and intimate."

FRENCH 75

~~~~~~~~~~~~~~~~~~~~~~~~~

LAGUNA BEACH, CA

Design ◗ Hatch Design Group, Costa Mesa, CA
Photography ◗ Scott Rothwall

A highlight of the place is the mural over the bar in the vaulted lounge. Based on Hatch's research, monkeys were used as a popular decorative motif in the 1930s so he had a local artist paint a "battle scene" between capering monkeys and cute cherubs. The battle is over champagne—the featured drink at the bar. The bar is separated from the main dining room by heavy velvet drapery.

The name? French 75 doesn't refer to a year but to a big cannon developed by the French in WW I. It was later used in WW II and then popularized as a drink that combines champagne with cognac and lemon juice.

THE CAFÉ

HEAL'S, LONDON, U.K.

Design ▪ Virgile & Stone Associates, Ltd., London

To design The Café at Heal's flagship store on Tottenham Court Rd. in London, the designers, Virgile & Stone, opted for a design concept that was "contemporary with a timeless, enduring quality which embraces the spirit and ethos of Heal's." To accomplish this they combined good design and craftsmanship with quality materials. The Café's appeal had to be broad: a relaxed and informal setting for breakfast, brunch, lunch and afternoon tea.

The entrance is defined by two large, dark veneered panels to either side of the door which contrasts with the white walls of the furniture department where The Café is located. The logo and highlighted menu boxes are finished in stainless steel. To create additional seating, the service bar was relocated to a central point. Made of curved dark timber and topped with stainless steel, the beverage bar acts as a focal point. The windows that run along one side are screened off by white oak louvered panels which are backlit. The area is also defined by "U" shaped, loose bench seating which is upholstered in taupe colored leather and matching colored

tiles are set in the floor. Sliding wall panels, lacquered aubergine, can be used to screen off part of the space for private dining/parties. When not in use, they fold back into a specially designed cupboard recessed in the wall.

The soft color palette combines white oak with dark stained timber, taupe leather and floor tiles and accents of aubergine and pale blue. Located within niches in the purple toned wall panels are specially commissioned photographs of Heal's products. To overcome the effect of the existing low ceilings, mirrors are used to "create a sense of light and space, and lighting (was used) to enhance the linear effect." A metal trough in the ceiling contains moveable spotlights that accent the table top settings. The custom loose bench seating also allows for more intimate seating arrangements in the space.

Within a limited budget and a tight time frame, the work was accomplished . The store remained open and function and there was minimal disruption to the customer's comfort or service.

SOHO SPICE

~~~~~~~~~~~~~~~~~~~~~~

SOHO, LONDON, U.K.

Design ▪ Fitch Design Consultants, London, U.K.

According to Fitch, the design firm for the new restaurant with fusion cuisine of oriental and occidental flavorings, Soho Spice has "all of the raw vibrancy that is village India with its riot of blazing colour—a tribute to the exotic palette of the sub-continent."

Located on Wardour St. in Soho, a theater and entertainment filled district of London, Amin Ali's new cafe will appeal to the younger, creative professionals who live and work there. To execute Ali's concept, Fitch responded with a stunning use of color combined with an honest, artisanal approach that is evocative of the arts and crafts of rural India.

Spice is the theme! Spice is carried through in seasoning the food and in the colors around the presented foods. The restaurant facade displays strong images of spices and in the windows antique spice jars from Livingstone's botanical expeditions are on display. Inside, the bar is below ground level and the restaurant/cafe is at street level. Throughout, the walls are divided into upper and lower portions and they are exuberant in bright blues, saffrons, paprika, sage and other raw—but brilliant—spice inspired colors. The same bold palette is applied to the tables and chairs that furnish each of the several connected and interacting spaces. The wood floors have been stained to go with the "feature spice colour" of the particular area. The ground floor eating area is "cool" with viridian, aqua and mint green applied in unique combinations. In blazing contrast is the basement bar area which pulsates with splashes of paprika, chili and saffron—"its intense hues both stimulating and cocooning." The supporting columns are incorporated into the spice story in the cafe. They are trimmed with framed pictures of spices and Indian art and there is a deliberate randomness to the placement and application of the artwork. The stories of the specific spices are told on vivid cards that are attached to the menus—each spice has been beautifully photographed to capture the essence of the subject. The patrons are invited to take the spice cards with them—as souvenirs and as part of a collection of 12 different cards.

The graphics on the cards and the menus "bring a reflection of the everyday written Hindi to the Western alphabet, the clean typography contrasting with a rough patterning that is representative of the meeting of East and West." The design of the 200 seat cafe/bar is also an "imaginative mingling of the clean lines of contemporary Soho with the rougher, more authentic hurley-burley of Indian village life."

turmeric root

The brilliant yellow one. Sunshine bright as a vegetable dye, useful as an antiseptic, exotic in perfume and a luminous, pungent ingredient of curry powder. Turmeric can also be used to make a paper which will disclose alkalis and acids by its changing colour.

SOHO
SPICE
BAR · CAFE · TANDOOR
124–126 Wardour St
Soho London W1V 3LA
T 0171 434 0808
F 0171 434 0799
Email info@sohospice.co.uk
Internet www.sohospice.co.uk

fennel

The philanderer's herb. Traditionally it was believed to be an aphrodisiac and symbol of sexual licence, but rather dangerously for women it was also an emblem of flattery. Not all is bad though - fennel makes a great breath freshener.

SOHO
SPICE
BAR · CAFE · TANDOOR
124–126 Wardour St
Soho London W1V 3LA
T 0171 434 0808
F 0171 434 0799
Email info@sohospice.co.uk
Internet www.sohospice.co.uk

MOLYVOS

〜〜〜〜〜〜〜〜〜〜

SEVENTH AVE., NEW YORK, NY

Design ▪ Morris Nathanson Design, Pawtucket, RI
Photography ▪ Warren Jagger, Providence

Molyvos is situated on Seventh Ave. between 55th and 56th Streets—a bit north but still very much a part of NYC's theater district and not too far from Carnegie Hall. The design team under the direction of Morris Nathanson was called upon to renovate an existing restaurant. They added some Hellenic details to the existing building facade and introduced a typical Greek parapet over the cornice— "creating an appropriate storefront complete with doors and side panels that are authentic Greek."

The most casual part of Molyvos is the small café to the left of the entrance. It is located between the bar and the sidewalk. Here, the banquettes that line the wall are upholstered in typical Byzantine or Middle East style tapestry fabrics and mirrors are used to open up the space. The bar is to the left. The original bar was kept but artisans and craftspersons transformed it by distressing the surfaces and a rolled copper top was added. The back bar was treated with a very classic faux finish and pendant lights hang over the bar. The original floor tiles were replaced with tiles in the Greek earth colors of terra cotta and black and these define the bar area. A large "drink royal" was erected opposite the bar to separate the seated guests from the stand-up bar patrons. The bench design that is used here adds to the casual ambiance of the space. A booth, made in island-style construction, serves to divide the bar from the main dining room. The designers created a cove area to conceal the connection between the restaurant and the hotel lobby and yet maintain a smooth traffic flow. The construction also serves as a major service station.

The restaurant has a new wood floor and the walls have a faux bois finish on the lower part which has been "aged and glazed." The upper walls are mottled and sponged to achieve a "sense of vintage" throughout the space. All the lighting was carefully researched to add "authenticity to the space." The raised dining room platform was extended and the floor is carpeted. The walls, here, are sponged a light salmon/terra cotta color which becomes an ideal background for the collection of memorabilia and artifacts. The artwork on the wainscot that surrounds the major columns was inspired by an artifact that John Livanos, the owner, brought back from Greece. The seating on the platform is most flexible.

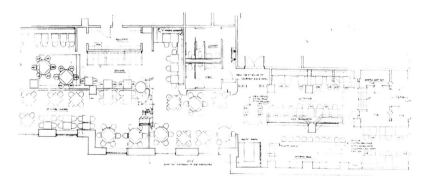

Throughout, the restaurant is enriched with vintage photographs of the island of Lesvos and the village of Molyvos, memorabilia and typical Greek artifacts. All of this is in honor of John Liivanos and his family who grew up and lived in the fishing village of Molyvos. Molyvos, the restaurant, has garnered rave reviews not only for the Greek cuisine but for the setting. Gael Greene, writing in New York Magazine said, "Suddenly the space has come alive with photos of the family and island life, ceramics, and folk art, the classic patterns of Greek tiles, rough stenciling and mottled terra cotta walls."

OCEANA

~~~~~~~~~~~~~~~~~~~~~~~~~~~~~

LONDON, U.K.

Design ▪ Fitch, London

What to do when the available space is in a basement and not only is there no daylight—there are no windows? Fitch, the London based design consulting firm was faced with this enigma when they were approached by Tony Kitous, a successful restaurateur, and challenged to solve it by creating a setting for Oceana, a new restaurant/café that serves a light Mediterranean, fish-based cuisine.

The result, illustrated here, is a bright, open and light contemporary space that has an underwater feeling without the sense of being submerged. The cool aqua, elliptically shaped light source, in the ceiling, along with the light aqua flooded columns add to the watery ambiance as do the blue, purple and moss green upholstered chairs. The walls and ceiling are crisp white and that also helps to overcome the below ground feeling. A rear wall repeats the aqua color and it is patterned in black with a Greek-like motif. As an accent there are deep red chairs mixed in with the cooler colored ones and there are red backed wall niches cut into the white textured walls. They become the "windows" in the window-less space and suggest that there is something beyond the thick walls. They also refer in a very clean and contemporary way to Mediterranean or Greek village architecture.

The lounge area is centered by the copper clad bar. A divider, also finished in copper, has a see-through cut-out and serves as a partition in the dining room. The violet and red barrel chairs surround miniature blond wood tables. Here, and throughout the restaurant, the floor is covered in white tiles which further tends to open up and lighten the space. Stainless steel hand rails and decoratives are used along with the previously mentioned copper units as accents. "The interior, created with a very light budget, features clean lines, careful detailing, and a Mediterranean inspired colour palette."

O L I V O

L O N D O N , U . K .

Design ▪ Pierluigi Piu, Architect, Cagliari, Italy
Photography ▪ Pierluigi Piu

What the owners of Olivo wanted was a design that would not have any of the pretentiousness that had overwhelmed the restaurant scene in the late 1980s and early 1990s. They wanted a setting for their cuisine that would have reference to their Mediterranean origins, to their traditions and to the nearly peasant gastronomic culture of their regions and "their common memory of childhood spent close to the sea." To execute this "dream," they called upon the architect/designer, Pierluigi Piu of Cagliari, Italy.

"From the decorative point of view, I decided to interpret the feelings of my clients by designing a place where any detail was meant to have the taste of the old, good ordinary things, of the old country houses or of the places of resort of any small Mediterranean province." The colors Piu used

were meant to evoke the sense of sun and sea. All the walls were plastered with lime, sand and natural pigments. The upper area is a warm yellow and the wainscot below is a full, strong ultramarine blue. The line where "sea and sun" meet is purposefully left soft and uneven. Above the blue dado is a decorative stenciled band that uses geometric shapes that are meant to suggest different forms and shapes of pasta. A skirting of terra cotta tiles band the base of the walls and the tiles are also used to frame the doors many of which are old, striped wood.

Wood is another dominant, decorative element used in Olivo. It is used around the front window like a giant picture frame. Just like the floor timbers, all the wood was stripped down to its natural color. The bar counter and chairs are also wood while the chair backs and seats are finished with raffia: a modern interpretation on an old Italian country chair. The presence of the restaurant on the street has been enhanced by the natural solid wood of the facade and the two stele forged of rusted iron. Seated atop the stele are laurel plants shaped into spheres. One pedestal also supports the café's menu board.

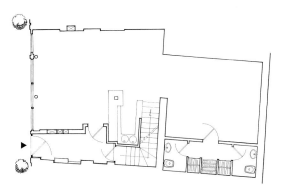

OLIVETO

Design ▪ Pierluigi Piu, Architect, Cagliari, Italy
Photography ▪ Pierluigi Piu

This new, small Italian restaurant which seats 50 was designed by Pierluigi Piu, an architect/designer from Cagliari, Italy. It was designed to complement Olivo, a larger restaurant he created for the same owner. The architect was greatly limited by the small space and what structural changes he did make were all done to add a feeling of space where it did not exist.

The facade was redesigned and opened up to gain maximum transparency. It was painted lime green "which is very appealing to the trendy clientele of Chelsea." The small lobby leads to the dining room as well as the staircase that brings guests up to the waiting room and toilets upstairs. To make this front area appear larger, the partition between the lobby and the restaurant was replaced by a full length, glazed panel. The street level is comprised of a bar area and two main dining rooms. The overall space is characterized by the "boiserie" on the walls: full length panels of veneered white maple decorated with an overlay pattern of oversized silhouettes of olive twigs. The upper

part of each panel is left natural and the lower portion is stained brown—as a reference to the Mediterranean soil. The floor is laid with "mat granito-gres" tiles of a light sand color. Each tile has been broken into several pieces before being laid to achieve a "craquelee" pattern.

Custom, long wood benches, designed by the architect, stretch along the wall opposite the bar and they are covered with blue cushions that were made to look like old mattresses. The accompanying tables have mahogany tops and white maple turned legs with teal painted feet. The pull up chairs were designed by Philippe Starck and produced in Italy.

The bar has a white maple counter top and it partially rests on small turned aluminum feet. The back bar is fitted with a self supporting glass unit. Besides the bar is an opening that leads to the kitchen which is in the basement. This alcove is painted a dusty blue color and it is illuminated by three oblong lamps made of white translucent glass. The lighting in the dining areas is from overhead spots.

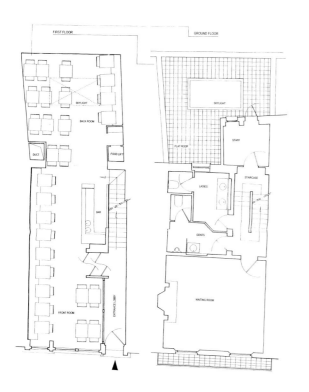

SARDUCCI'S

TORONTO, CANADA

Design ▪ Hirschberg Design Group, Toronto
Photography ▪ Richard Johnson, Interior Images

By combining "simple elegance and European hospitality," the designers, Hirschberg Design Group of Toronto, established the look for Sarducci's as "an innovative and exciting dining experience."

There are six distinct areas in Sarducci's: a café, a retail area, an open kitchen, a bar, a patio and the dining room. With the completely open kitchen as the focal point of the design, the space is a lively mix of juxta-posed colors and textures that create "a contemporary version of rustic country." This ambiance is attractive to all age groups.

The palette is rich in earthy colors like ocher, pompeian red, amber and green. The walls are faux painted—heavy on texture—and rendered to appear streaked and weathered. By changing the color of the walls, the enclosing spaces seem to dissolve into one another. Long, timber outlined

openings in some of the partition dividers seem like windows that open up to the space beyond. The designers made effective use of these enlarged window openings "to separate the space while maintaining privacy for the patrons" as well as accent the 14-ft. ceiling height of the space. The open ceiling—full of corrugated metal panels, pipes, ducts and vents—is painted a light color and suspended down from it are conical shaped lamps of different designs.

In the less "formal" areas the tables and chairs are painted in the same palette as that used on the walls and the mismatched tables and chairs are grouped in mix- and don't-match clusters on the almost white tile floor. The high backed booths, set along one of the perimeter walls, are upholstered in a print fabric. In the café/bar the wood covered walls are stained a gray tone and the banquette is covered in black and teal with aqua and coral toss pillows added to complement the yellow on the pull-up chairs and the cocktail tables.

Throughout there are bright, fun, framed paintings and small artifacts set out on shelves projecting off the color stained walls. A highlight of the open display kitchen is the fieldstone encrusted wall oven which is set between ocher streaked and faded red wall panels. In another area, rather than the off-white floor tiles, the floor is carpeted in assorted colored and sized rectangles of red, green, black and gold: variations on the wall colors and the accents.

Involved in every stage of the project from developing a market strategy, working with the chef and the general contractor, the exterior and interior design as well as the cost analyzing, Hirschberg Design Group created a lively, inviting and color filled concept that sets Sarducci's apart from the rest.

LEVANTES

DUPONT CIRCLE, WASHINGTON, DC

Design ▪ Adamstein & Demetriou Architects, Washington, DC
Principals in charge ▪ Olvia Demetriou, AIA & Theodore Adamstein
Project Architect ▪ Lance Hosey AIA
Design Team ▪ Vanessa Kassabian
Photography ▪ Theodore Adamstein

Levantes features an Eastern Mediterranean cuisine that is presented in a new way and in a fresh environment which transforms the low ceilinged and L-shaped plan into a rich and enjoyable space to spend some time.

Most of the ceiling is now open to reveal the existing structure. The three main areas of the restaurant are defined by "dynamically shaped ceilings that appear to float in space." The bar and dining room are identified by two asymmetrical vaults which are connected by an "S"-shaped soffit. This suggests the "wave" in the Levantes logo. The dining room vault centers over a tile clad hearth which contains a wood burning oven.

In creating the color palette for Levantes, Adamstein & Demetriou, the architects/designers, used colors that reflect the traditional architecture and palette of the Levantine region. The Mediterranean sea and sky is represented by the deep blues in the tilework and in the fabrics. Bright yellow recalls sunlight while the creamy stucco surfaces pick up on the Levantine building vernacular. Cycladic Island architecture is also suggested by the vaulted ceilings and the deep wall niches. Natural stone and wood finishes are used throughout.

Creating an "evocative backdrop" for the outdoor café is the bar which features a back bar accented by a large sheet of amber colored glass which is backlit. It is suspended against a blue, glass tiled wall. Again, they reiterate the blue/yellow or sea/sun colors of Levantes.

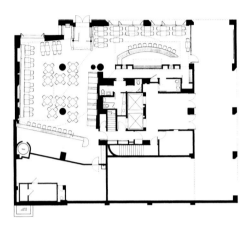

NACIONAL 27

CHICAGO, IL

Design ▪ Lieber Cooper Associates, Chicago
Gerardo Fitz Gibbons
Photography ▪ Steinkamp & Ballogg, Chicago

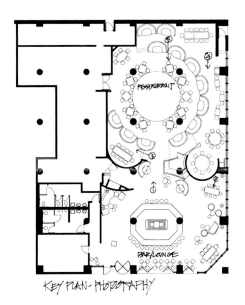

KEY PLAN-PHOTOGRAPHY

acional 27, set in Chicago's River North, is another successful restaurant concept for Lettuce Entertain You enterprises. With this design by Lieber Cooper Associates of Chicago, they "explore the nuances of Latin and South American cuisine and night life" and they bring Latin dancing and dance music to the Midwest.

Gerardo Fitz Gibbons of the Lieber Cooper firm combined South Beach Miami and Cuban motifs to create a "nueva Latina" ambiance. The design team worked within modest budget constraints and a short time frame as much of the existing space as possible. They did create a very different look by adding partitions, using flowing white draperies on the walls and windows to suggest the Miami feeling, ambient lighting for the mood, accent lighting to highlight the artwork and tabletops and candlelight for an overall romantic glow.

The exterior carries a huge sign that serves as a beacon for the café and it is the only element that even suggests what lies beyond the frosted grid exterior bays of the commercial building. The radical floor plan, on the interior, is centered around a 20-ft. diameter bamboo dance floor. Using a "syncopated architectural geometry," the designers created a variety of private and semi-private dining spaces often just separated by the silky white draperies.

Semi-circular booths surround the dance floor along with free-standing tables. Also guarding the dance floor are four giant columns and a silver framed mirror-almost 12 feet in size—hangs on the wall and echoes images of the dancers and the diners.

To get to the dining area guests must pass by the octagonal shaped bar and lounge up front. The black bar is capped with a wood counter and extending up to the ceiling are the Brazilian-Modern inspired shelves that hold the wines and liquors. The bongo shaped bar stools are Afro-Caribbean in spirit. Adding to the relaxed charm of the lounge area are the soft, upholstered chairs and sofas, the flowing, ceiling-to-floor white draperies, the candlelight, and the graceful palm trees that are omnipresent.

Nacional 27—the name—salutes the 27 nations in Latin America from where the varied cuisine originated.

THE GRAND LUX CAFÉ

VENETIAN HOTEL/CASINO, LAS VEGAS, NV

Design ▪ Rick McCormick: V.P. Design for
Cheesecake Factory/David Overton: President/CEO,
Cheesecake Factory
Sr. Designer ▪ Teresa Kelly
Photography ▪ Berger/Conser Photography, Santa Monica

This is Italian with a twist. The twist is in the execution and in the "Venetian" setting in Las Vegas. The Grand Lux Café is GRAND and LUX in every sense of either word and it is a magnificent addition to the Cheesecake Factory operation.

The guest leaves all sense of the commonplace behind as he or she enters through the magnificent shopfront which is finished in finely crafted mahogany and burlwood and the woods are complemented by the fresco paintings above and the handblown glass lighting sconces. Once through the glamorous arches, the guest is surrounded by a Renaissance renaissance with tromp l'oeil murals on the vaulted ceilings and the fragrance emanating from the bakery. The bakery is "an interesting marriage of contemporary and classical details." There are back lit, Venetian glass panels set in mahogany framework and swirling patterns of mosaic tiles embedded in the rich, red wood counter.

In the bar/lounge of the Café, the guest is inundated with details, jewel-like colors of glass tiles and polished stainless steel. The mosaics are used to pattern the walls to either side of the mahogany bar whose front is also enriched with the colorful glass tiles. The walls are covered with gold leaf and the dark stained, wood, coffered ceiling complements the rich glowing gold of the walls. There are high backed booths covered in a jewel toned print fabric as well as leather pull-up chairs with backs covered with strips of brown leather and seats upholstered in gold leather. Amber glass wall and column sconces illuminate the space with a warm, rich golden aura.

Along the way to the Grand Dining Room there are marble floors inlaid with "tumbled marble medallions that express the rich gold and terra cotta colors of Italy." The dining room is an experience! The cathedral scale ceilings are adorned with gold relief garlands and the soffits seem to be covered with luxurious salmon colored suede. The overscaled columns in this room are finished in a high gloss mahogany and garnished with an ornate, gold leaf crown molding. These lead the eye towards the richly colored murals. "The wall murals at the wall twinkles and radiates due to the metallic paints used on the canvas." Like a grand stage—befitting the grandeur and scale of the

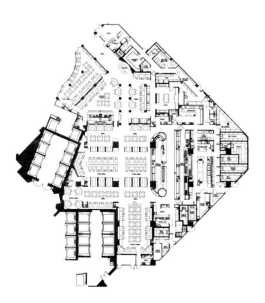

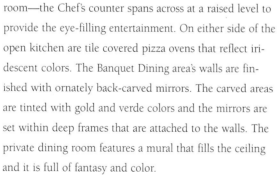

room—the Chef's counter spans across at a raised level to provide the eye-filling entertainment. On either side of the open kitchen are tile covered pizza ovens that reflect iridescent colors. The Banquet Dining area's walls are finished with ornately back-carved mirrors. The carved areas are tinted with gold and verde colors and the mirrors are set within deep frames that are attached to the walls. The private dining room features a mural that fills the ceiling and it is full of fantasy and color.

Throughout this 20,000 sq. ft. Italian Renaissance inspired wonderland all the light fixtures were custom designed and produced including the chandeliers with the hand blown, studio glass trim in a variety of colors and shapes. These lighting units are enlivened with hand forged ironwork. When in Venice—Las Vegas style—don't miss dining in the Grand Lux manner

SPIGA RISTORANTE

SCARSDALE, NY

Design ▪ Haverson Architecture & Design, Greenwich, CT

Photography ▪ Paul Warchol Photography

In order to create Spiga Ristorante, located on a busy main drive in Scarsdale, NY, the team of Haverson Architecture & Design of Greenwich, CT, found it necessary to gut the 5500 sq. ft. existing space in order to affect an open and inviting café. Walls and columns were redefined, new roofing was applied and exterior signage was added. They also designed a playful new logo using teal, sienna, verde, umber, plum and midnight blue: the same palette that plays an important part in the interior design scheme and the ceiling mural.

As the diner enters there is a low, flat ceiling space decorated with a mottled, midnight blue sky. The custom accent lights—whimsically shaped like stars and moon—punctuate the dark ceiling and add to the illusion of a Tuscan night sky. "The ceiling at the entry conveys a sense of illusion and acts as a prelude to the romantic daytime mural in the main space." The chiaroscuro ceiling mural by Tom Glissen depicting a dreamy Italian landscape is the focus of the interior.

A strong diagonal play of planes—"slashing, leaning columns"—frame the perimeter of the dining area with canted railings set in between. Directing the guest into the 175-seat room are the series of facade-like banquettes that seem to form an angled wall. In the composition there are three representative scale elements that suggest the image of shopfronts on a street that forms a boundary to a piazza. To intensify the "festival-like surroundings," the designers have specified colorful surfaces and decorative finishes. Faux textured walls in ocher and soft green are complemented by bold accents of earthy reds. A brilliant streak of red-violet makes a sinuous sweep over the bar. The bar, itself, was salvaged from an earlier restaurant and it has a drink rail and displays, on its front, a platinum colored, tufted diamond design.

There is a strategically placed pizza oven and another focal highlight is the food display on a distressed copper surface. The display is surrounded by a mosaic of cracked tiles and it is covered with flush mahogany panels set at a 30 degree angle "to create a visual sense of extension and a seemingly larger space."

In explaining his design, Jay Haverson said, "I took real images of Tuscany and made them dream-like and more distinctive,"

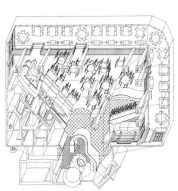

CASTALDI'S MARKET & GRILL

HUNTERSVILLE, NC

Design ▪ Little & Associates, Architects, Charlotte, NC
Senior Designer & Project Manager ▪ Steve Starr
Design Team ▪ Josh Cool/Jeanne Mercer/Linda Kratz
Photography ▪ Stanley Capps

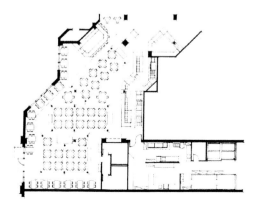

Castaldi's Market & Grill, in Huntersville, NC, is a division of, and was designed by, Little & Associates, Architects of Charlotte, NC. The design proves you can have the best of two choices in one space: eat in or take it home. The concept behind this "market and grill" is that a shopper can dine in on a fabulous Italian menu in a rich, atmospheric setting or take out a fully prepared meal from the market place. This brings "HMR" (home meal replacement) to a new height in refinement. Working with Neil Castaldi, who remembers the open air markets of his childhood in a town near Naples, the architects designed this 220-seat, upscale, casual restaurant. Here "the colorful produce, the perfume of the herbs, and the festive sound all blend together to create a symphony for the senses."

The market area in the 5000 sq. ft. space is rich in textures, colors and aromas. Dark woods are accented by the gleaming metal trim of the illuminated refrigerator cases, the copper pots and pans suspended over the open, exhibition kitchen where all the foods are prepared, the dozens of wicker and raffia baskets laden with delicacies, strings of garlic, and delicate dripping lights over the food displayed on the cases. Signs over the long, multi-angled serving counter indicate what can be purchased where. The heavy plank wood floors contribute to the old world ambiance.

For the dine-in diner, the European market place theme carries over. The mahogany colored chairs and white linen covered tables are set out under billowing canvas "tent tops"—like those that flap and add such color to the open air markets. Piercing the sheets and dropping through them are deep red metal shaded lamps while dozens of "supporting" poles angle up diagonally from the floor to catch the canvas sails.

The wine bar becomes another focal point with a back bar filled with nested wine bottles. At the rear of the space, above the deep green painted wainscot is a colorful collage of posters, labels and memorabilia. recessed into an arch

on the ocher-gold wall, Adding to the festive look of the space are the harvest tables that replace the traditional wait stations. Castaldi's Market & Grill has already opened replicas of this concept in Charlotte, NC, Roanoke, VA, and Detroit, MI.

V A S C O

~~~~~~~~~~~

M I L L   V A L L E Y ,   C A

Design ▪ Backen Arrigoni Ross, San Francisco, CA
Principal ▪ Richard Beard
Architect ▪ Charlie Theobold
Project Administrator ▪ Eric Stockman
Photography ▪ Douglas Dunn, San Francisco, CA

In creating the 2000 sq. ft., 60-seat, café/bar, Pasul Lazzarescchi, the owner, was paying homage to his father, Vasco. Located in the heart of Mill Valley, this warm and honest space was designed by Backen Arrigoni Ross of San Francisco. The building is situated on a corner and the architects reconfigured the entrance and enlarged the existing windows to "marry the outside street activity with the inside of the restaurant."

Inside there are three zones. An intimate and friendly neighborhood bar is located up front and a wood burning pizza oven and rotisserie dominates the far opposite end of the space. In between are simple tables and chairs set out on the natural wood floor. Banquettes, upholstered in a subtle striped fabric, run the length between the bar and the counter set out in front of the ovens. The wood paneled and plastered walls are adorned with the artwork of local artists as well as photos relevant to Vasco's life.

The rotisserie is located inside a brick covered alcove and the white tile faced pizza oven is in a nearby curved enclosure that is finished in a faux texture of ocher and umber. The plaster walls are also textured to contrast with the smooth, red/orange wood that is used throughout. The bar/counter in front of the open kitchen can seat six on soft, mossy green covered stools. The same moss green material is used on the loose seating in the café and combined with a faded blue in a vertical stripe on a natural background it upholsters the banquette backs. The ceiling is coffered by beams criss-crossing across the plaster ceiling. From the ceiling drop, white translucent shaded lamps provide the ambient light. Smaller replicas appear on the divider partition that runs the length of the dining area.

The bar, at the entrance is almost a replica of the one at the kitchen end. Here, however, the back bar is lined up with shelves filled with wines and liquors.

CELADON

NEW YORK, NY

Design ▪ Bogdanow Partners, Architects, P.C., New York
Design Team ▪ Larry Bogdanow/Keary Horiuchi/
Warren Ashworth/Tina Lai
Photography ▪ Courtney Grant Winston

East meets West at Celadon, a new, 4400 sq. ft. restaurant on upper Madison Ave. in NYC. The owner, Yangjoon Moi, wanted a café/restaurant that would reflect the subtle mix of Asian and International cuisine. The resulting design by Bogdanow Partners of NYC is a cool and sparkling space that like its name, Celadon, blends Asian with California sensibilities and attitudes. "The palette evokes the delicate green of Chinese porcelain, accented with silver, champagne and soft earth tones, imbuing the restaurant with a peaceful and warm ambiance."

The "inviting café" setting on the ground level of this two level restaurant can be seen through the large windows of the facade. The flooring, here, is a mix of maple wood and golden quartzite which combines beautifully with the elegantly patterned, upholstered dining chairs. The soft, gentle coloring and the overall seating plan creates a "salon-like" atmosphere in this space.

A stainless steel and glass elevator, almost centered in the space, leads to the second level of Celadon. The open stairway together with the elevator are "designed in the spare and elegant vocabulary of the space" and contribute to the Asian feel of the space. From the main dining room, on the upper level, there is a panoramic view of Madison Ave. and, at night, the room is softly illuminated by custom torcheres. Lending a "dynamic energy" to the space are the undulating sculptural banquettes which are upholstered in earth toned, sueded fabrics. There is also a private dining room on this level which features a pyramidal shaped ceiling over the silk-screened wall coverings. The wainscoting is warm, cherry wood.

The cool serene lower level with its bowl shaped, hanging ceiling lights and its gentle palette is complemented by the rich, earthy and terra cotta colors of the upper level.

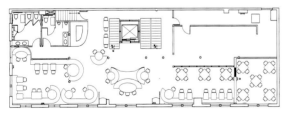

1 Second Floor Plan

2 First Floor Plan

O N D I N E

S A U S O L I T O, C A

Design ▪ Engstrom Design Group, San Rafael, CA
Photography ▪ Cesar Rubio

There was a time, in the 1960s and 1970s, when dining at Ondine on the Sausolito waterfront, was an occasion. However, times had changed. Engstrom Design Group of San Rafael, CA was called upon by the California Café Restaurant Corp. to "resurrect this culinary landmark" and update the 4600 sq. ft. space and bring it into the 21st century. The designers took their inspiration from the café's location and the chef's eclectic menu which is a blend of the flavors of Asia, the Mediterranean and California.

The seating is creatively oriented around the large picture windows which surround three sides of the restaurant. This provides diners with unrestricted vistas that extend from the Sausolito waterfront and Angel Island to the Bay Bridge, East Bay and the fascinating San Francisco skyline. The adventure starts in the 17-ft. high circular entry with its undulating wooden trellises. From here one can go up to the small bar that seats 15. It is reached via a gently curving ramp and the bar overlooks the main dining space.

The dining room can accommodate 108 guests in the Pullman booths and dining tables that are nestled against the low and high walls that run parallel to the windows. The designers selected a rich and textured palette to furnish and finish Ondine. Venetian plaster with integrated

color has been applied to the walls in a dramatic set of colors that range from butterscotch to terra cotta and plum. The woodwork is a combination of mahogany and spotted bubinga from Africa. In the bar area, Japanese-style, distressed and recycled plank flooring was used. For the upholstery fabrics, the designers selected a patchwork that combines Asian and Mediterranean inspired materials.

Separating the dining room from the bar is an open, decorative divider made of fine hardwoods and textured metals. Geometric iron railings that suggest an art deco source are used and the wrought iron sconces, between the large windows, add "architectural interest." Throughout Ondine one sees and feels the work of the local artisans who have contributed so much to the uniqueness of the finished project.

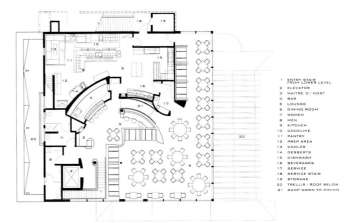

1 ENTRY STAIR
  FROM LOWER LEVEL
2 ELEVATOR
3 MAITRE 'D / HOST
4 BAR
5 LOUNGE
6 DINING ROOM
7 WOMEN
8 MEN
9 KITCHEN
10 COOKLINE
11 PANTRY
12 PREP AREA
13 COOLER
14 DESSERTS
15 DISHWASH
16 BEVERAGES
17 SERVICE
18 SERVICE STAIR
19 STORAGE
20 TRELLIS / ROOF BELOW
21 RAMP DOWN TO DINING

ONDINE RESTAURANT

3 0 1

SAN FRANCISCO, CA

Design ▪ Studio Architectura/MBH Architects,
San Rafael, CA
Design Team ▪ Shawn Alexander/Clay Fry/
Ken Lidicker/Donald Hadsell
Photography ▪ Dennis Anderson Photography, San Rafael

Within a space of 2000 sq. ft. and intimate seating for 65, 301 is located on the ground level of a newly renovated, six story, residential loft project on the edge of the Embarcadero. It is in San Francisco's "South of Market" up and coming neighborhood. The subtle yet unmistakably Pan-Asian ambiance represents a collaborative effort of client, architect, designers and artisans. "Like the chefs who have created Asian Fusion food, the collective team put together an interior immersed in watery motifs that are recognizable as Asian but does not specifically refer to any one country."

The entry accesses into the bar. The most striking element here is the iron railing "sculpted to look like the tendrils of kelp growing up out of the floor to wrap around the railings." The ceiling is raw concrete and the pale anigre bar is capped with granite and bamboo. Ceramic vases are displayed in niches and the iron and wicker stools continue the Pan-Asian imagery. The 65-seat dining room is separated from the bar by a 30-ft. long waterfall. Further evoking images of the East is the light but tough flooring of bamboo. Though there are no windows in this café, the teak stained, wooden louvers on the wall suggest windows in a tropical plantation house and thus unseen vistas beyond. Raw concrete columns with mushroom shaped

caps that were poured to match pre-existing columns elsewhere in the building "keep the material quality of the space honest, and work well, in counterpoint, with the upholstery fabrics in leather and silk and the gentle moss and creamy tones of the walls." The lovely custom designed lily pad light fixtures, made of silk stretched over iron frames, "conjure up a generalized Pacific Rim ambiance."

Focal points in the dining room are the tall Emperor's throne banquette at the rear of the space. It can seat three. A statue of Buddha stands watch over the space while the neatly gridded wall niches show off a collection of elegant ceramic vases. The brightly lit boxiness of the niches complements the soft circles of light that emanate from the lily pad lights.

OBECA-LI

~~~~~~

TRIBECA, NEW YORK, NY

Design ▪ Bogdanow Partners, P.C., New York
Photography ▪ Courtney Grant Winston

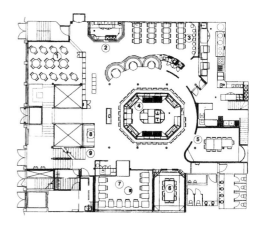

This three level, 14,000 sq. ft. Japanese restaurant was created in what was formerly a church for Li Ping in the "in" neighborhood of Tribeca in NYC. As envisioned and fully realized by Bogdanow Partners, Architects, it is a refuge of peace and quiet in a very unpeaceful and not too quiet world.

To fully understand what the client wanted, Larry Bogdanow joined Li Ping in a whirlwind tour of Japan where they saw, they sampled, and sipped every form of food service from noodle shops and sushi bars to robato-yaki bars, saki bars, tea houses and ultra chic restaurants. The resulting research ended up in the layout of the large space which has been gracefully divided into private tatami dining rooms, a spare sushi bar on the lower level, several open dining rooms on the main level and a saki bar on the upper level.

After passing by the waterfall at the entrance and beyond the exotic foliage, the guests cross over a wooden bridge, on the main level, and are faced with a variety of offerings. There is the main dining room and the more private Moon Gate room as well as a private tatami room, or the guests can choose to visit the Kobachi Bar. Here, 30 seats surround the open display kitchen and there are three semi-circular booths that are a part of—yet apart from—the kitchen where guests can still see the action. Natural wood floors, light wood tables and chairs, light neutral fabrics and a sinuous wood "fence" contains the Kobachi Bar. Throughout, this area is accented by the crenelated cast iron support columns that are painted black. Other options on the main level are the Tono booth which has a long table. From this location diners can see and be seen.

The Tatami Room is a warm and intimate room perfect for a private party of twelve. Rather than sitting on the floor, the floor has been recessed and the low seats have backs. According to Li Ping, the traditional Japanese elements were blended with the contemporary to make the place more comfortable for her customers. "I wanted 60 percent western and 40 percent Asian to appeal to my American, European and Asian customers."

The Saki Bar is located on the upper level and here the designers mixed eastern and western sensibilities to create a warm, lush setting that is truly unique. Throughout Obeca Li the design is a blend of opposites. There are the antique cast iron columns mixed with laminated rice paper screens and aluminum frames. Slat wood screens are left natural but the exposed HVAC system in the Saki Bar has been painted red. According to Larry Bogdanow, "What we added was Asian but left what was there— things that were loft-like—and some woodworking, textures and detailing."

THUNDER GRILL

WASHINGTON, DC

Design ▪ Adamstein & Demetriou Architects,
Washington, DC
Principals ▪ Olvia Demetriou, AIA/Theodore Adamstein
Architect ▪ Ira Tattelman
Photography ▪ Theodore Adamstein

Ark Restaurant Corporation of NYC took the Mainliner down to Washington, DC and not only got off at Union Station, they staked a space in that beautifully renovated terminal for their new venture in Southwestern cuisine. Designed by Adamstein & Demetriou Architects, of Washington DC, the concept for the interior of Thunder Grill focuses on the rich history of the American Southwest and it celebrates the cultures of Native Americans, Mexicans, and Americans. "Our intent was to create a place where you could feel the sensuality of Pueblo structures and cultures overlaid with the transient, expansive and powerful architecture of the American West."

The interior has been "sculpted" to provide a fabulous and exciting sense of height and breadth. "We have created bold architectural elements and forms from a variety of surfaces and textures that evoke the spirit of the Southwest, from towering adobe-like wall fragments at the entry hall, to the shotgun railroad structure that looms over the bar, to the magical and massive chili peppers that hang precariously over one's head. You become saturated in visual references that are presented in a surrealistic way."

The rectangular bar is faced with native stone and wood and it supports a zinc counter top. An armature of stained, rough-hewn wood outlines the bar in the soaring, double height space. The weathered wood planked floor adds to the Southwest ambiance as do the rough textured, adobe walls. A simple, open, black metal stairway connects the two dining levels and the giant, red chili pepper lanterns, by Donna Reinsel of Baltimore, bridges the space. They are hung from the vaulted ceiling that is most evident in the upper dining area and they descend down to about seven feet from the street level floor. Huge, decaying logs are suspended beneath the vaulting as are black lighting rods that end with halide lamps that help to illuminate the space. Other illumination is provided by swagged strings of monopoint spots, standing torchere lamps and mini lamps that stand and outline the zinc bar top.

Adding to the Southwest imagery are the intricate turquoise mosaic glass panels, the natural rough red stone that captures the sunset colors of the local cliffs, and the artwork on the table tops. The total design is "whimsical and evocative, sensual and exciting."

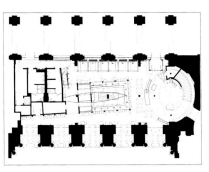

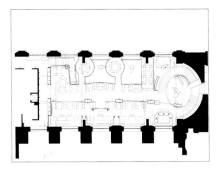

COYOTE GRILL

SCOTTSDALE, AZ

Design ▪ Exclaim! Design, Phoenix, AZ

The design challenge was to create an interesting setting for the new, 220–260 seat restaurant which is located in a retail and office space location. The solution was an indoor/outdoor bar dining area which effectively draws the diners in. The design of the building is Southwestern which reflects on the location as well as on the menu and the space is divided into a bar/lounge and a dining area. Seating in the bar can be used for additional dining space when needed. A separate smoking room has also been included in the space layout.

Though Southwestern finishes and materials are used, the design firm, Exclaim! of Phoenix, included copper panels and copper "moon" disks that float over the private dining room. Curved elements appear throughout as do colorful mosaic tiles, wood peeler logs and natural stone. The peeler logs are used in a unique manner: copper mesh panels are draped like canvas between the logs. "This not only gives an interesting play of light with the metal, but also creates a grand statement at the entry." The client wanted the ceiling exposed to affect the feeling of greater volume but thus caused problems with the acoustics and the lighting. The designers solved the problem by "lowering the ceiling" in the private dining areas. This was accomplished by dropping large, custom copper disks ("moons") from the exposed ceiling thus visually creating more intimate spaces.

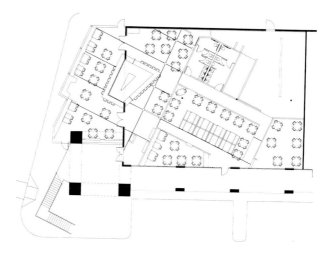

omo's is the brainchild of the San Francisco restaurateur, Peter Osborne, and his vision was realized by Studio Architectura & MBH Architects in the South Beach area of San Francisco. It is located opposite the very new Giant's Stadium in Pacific Bell Park. The restaurant/café is "the quintessence of both a high class restaurant and a genteel men's club."

The overall design attitude of the 10,000 sq. ft. space is "restrained and disciplined" to reveal an economy of materials and function, both of which are inherent in the San Francisco Waterfront vernacular. To suggest the simple "arts & crafts" influence, the major material palette includes wood, metal, iron, glass and textiles. The existing loading dock and parking area were raised to form a concrete platform that acts as a plinth for the building. A metal and glass canopy extends out over the entrance and the vestibule doors. Inside, the calm, quiet and neutral space is organized into three zones. The main dining room, which can accommodate 190 guests, is bordered by tufted, brown leather banquette seating and the faux textured, ocher-gold walls are accentuated by the light from the amber hanging lamps. Adding to that are the rich, reddish brown carpet underfoot. The overall effect is warm

M O M O ' S

~~~~~~~~~~~~~~~~~

S A N   F R A N C I S C O ,   C A

Architecture/Design ▪ Studio Architectura & MBH Architects, Alameda, CA
Design Team ▪ John McNulty: Principal/Shawn Alexander & Denis Heath: Principals, with: Clay Fry/Denise Darrin/Donald Hadsell
Photography ▪ Dennis Anderson Photography, San Rafael, CA

and welcoming. There is a subsidiary dining area that can function as a separate party room. Very visible behind the row of mahogany clad columns is the exhibition kitchen which is framed by a series of low arches. The amber glass down-lights play up the zinc counter top and the tile covered oven and work area behind.

The cherry wood and stainless steel bar, in the bar area up front, helps to create the "sophisticated ambiance" that carries through the rest of the space. The pianist's music carries through to the small banquet room and the main dining room as well as, weather permitting, the front patio which can be set up for dining.

Vintage posters and large framed photos of famous Giant baseball players add accents of color and enhance the warm, classic and masculine feeling of the design.

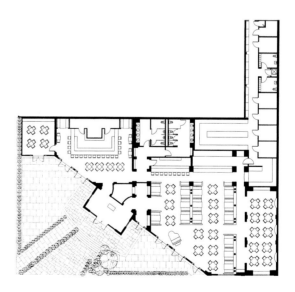

HOME TURF SPORTS BAR

LAS VEGAS, NV

Design ▪ AAD, Scottsdale, AZ
Photography ▪ Michael Norton, Norton Photography

Working closely with the Host Marriott Services Corporation, AAD of Scottsdale AZ designed the 3500 sq. ft. Home Turf Sports Bar in the main airport in Las Vegas. The design firm revitalized an existing bar facility into something new and different by combining National Football League material, high technology and the warmth and camaraderie of a local, neighborhood tavern. The new Home Turf Sports Bar is "an exciting, vibrant and comfortable facility for the weary traveler" where he or she can get away from the bustle and hustle of a busy airport.

Four X Four and multiple monitors are everywhere. They are a major design element of the space. No matter where a visitor may sit, there is always a clear view of the televised action. The entire café has been organized into areas of intimate seating through the subtle changes in floor levels and open partitions that divide but don't separate. Yet, the space retains the openness of a stadium or arena with the open grid ceiling and the translucent barricades that "create overall excitement." Brick walls, white tiles, yellow goal-posts and the black concrete floors with game strategy markings painted on them all add up to a "sports" set-

ting. The goal-posts define the assorted seating areas and the table tops are emblazoned with the logos of the different NFL teams. The NFL has also provided the memorabilia that is displayed throughout, thus creating a "sports museum" environment.

In addition to drinks and food service, there is a retail area where visitors can indulge in some NFL fantasies—and shopping. Branded merchandise from assorted NFL teams are presented in locker-like fixtures.

What used to be a "pick up and fly" kind of dining experience at airports is turning into a "sit down and relax" situation. Faced with revitalizing an existing restaurant facility, AAD of Scottsdale, AZ, provided a "fresh refuge" from the usual coming and going atmosphere one gets at airports into one that is an entertaining and relaxing experience.

The "diner" theme was selected for Arizona Roadhouse. It goes with the ever-increasing fascination people have with Americana, nostalgia and travel. The designers created what could be a diner—just off Rte 66—and the facade consists of an eclectic mix of artifacts, shapes, colors, and materials that "grab people's attention "and make the café stand out from the surrounding terminal. The signage emulates the car fins of an old, classic automobile and it invites weary travelers to come in, sit down, take it easy and enjoy "roadhouse grub."

Using clever graphics and thematic elements such as a menu board fashioned after a 1960s movie marquee, a hand-painted map mural and nostalgic trimmed table tops, the space takes on the feeling of a diner. Most of the "art" and artifacts that fill the space with interest and fun were collected by the design team as they followed Rte 66

ARIZONA ROADHOUSE

PHOENIX SKY HARBOR INTERNATIONAL AIRPORT, AZ

Design ▪ AAD, Scottsdale, AZ
Principal in charge ▪ Michael Stevenson, AIA
Principal Designer ▪ Carl F. Schaffer, AIA
Studio Director ▪ Doug Tener
Development Team ▪ Rob Burkhart/Jenn Reynolds/
Jarrod Tristan
Photography ▪ Michael Norton, Norton Photography.

through the many small towns along its way. The authentic 1936 red gas tank comes from Williams, and the rustic arrows were found in a trading post/truck stop outside of Flagstaff. "People have a love affair with cars and the most famous road ever built," said Carl Schaffer, the principal in charge of designing this project. "We had a strong palette of icons and imagery to work with in creating this truly unique airport dining experience."

A highlight of the 2600 sq. ft. café is the "drive-in" video screen which helps to further the concept of Arizona Roadhouse as an "entertaining pit stop along the traveler's cross country journey." The fun ambiance has been recognized with several design awards.

MYTHOS

~~~~~~~~~~~~~~~~~~~~~~~~~~~~~~~~~~~~~

ORLANDO, FL

Design ▪ Jordan Mozer & Associates, Chicago, IL.,
In collaboration with Universal Studios:
Mark Woodbury/Dale Mason/Eric Jany
Photography ▪ Doug Snower Photography, Chicago

Taking its imagery and decorative elements from the stories of Perseus and other Greek myths, Mythos is an all involving, all entertaining, 12,000 sq. ft. extravaganza set down in Universal Studios new theme park in Orlando, FL. It is on one of the five Islands of Adventure and, as designed by Jordan Mozer & Associates of Chicago in collaboration with a Universal Studio design team, it is "decorative magic."

Mythos is housed in what looks like an extinct volcano which has water cascading down its weathered and eroded slopes. The facade is "peopled" by Zeus, Narcissus who gazes down at his own image in the surrounding waters and Atlas who holds up the world. Inside it appears to be more like a sea cavern where the sinuous and textured walls have been "carved out and smoothed by centuries of surging waves." In the main dining room, the cavern's roof vaults skyward and through large openings, in the walls, diners look out onto a lagoon and a spacious outdoor seating area.

Subterranean streams run between the seating areas and the walls take on the shapes of "long vanished gods and their spirit minions." The Jordan Mozer signature elements are all there: the soft, flowing lines, the fabulous custom lighting fixtures that flame upward like amber torches, the elegantly detailed, pewter finished railings and the unexpected elements such as the unusual, tulip-backed banquettes upholstered in rich dubonnet fabric. A wonderful surprise is the sculpted dragon that slithers down one of the rocky walls to provide the "flames" for the pizza ovens. Theatrical lighting effects add mystical and magical touches throughout this fantastic environment. "The effect is only a step or two this side of awesome."

RICKENBAKERS BAR

COLORADO SPRINGS, CO

Design ▪ R D Jones & Associates, Baltimore, MD
Design Team ▪ Rebecca Jones/Cezar Gomez/
Cary Heefner/Karin Armstrong
Photography ▪ Whitney Cox

The Rickenbaker Bar and Lounge is situated adjacent to a 25,000 sq. ft. meeting area in the Sheraton Colorado Springs Hotel in Colorado. The theme that sets the look for this café/bar/disco is a salute to Eddie Rickenbaker who was a WW I pilot/hero. Thus, aviation history became the core concept, This decision was underscored by the hotel's location: very near the local airport and a large Air Force Academy.

In an attempt to appeal to both the young as well as the older guests, the designers introduced some 1940s and 1950s memorabilia which include a light fixture that resembles a juke box, black and white photos of '50s movie stars, old vinyl records, and a mural depicting big band musicians. Rebecca Jones, the designer, chose to include the nostalgic elements of the 1920s, the big band era of the '40s and the glamour of the movies of the '50s, because they would help to establish Rickenbaker's as a fun and playful place to be.

Jones divided the 1400 sq. ft. space into four cozy and inviting zones. There is the bar, the lounge, the concert/stage area and the game room. The bar is a friendly spot with strong colored flooring, mahogany accents, brighter lighting and an aviation themed mural at the outer edge of this space. The Lounge features soft lighting, plush upholstered chairs, a fireplace to add a feeling of warmth and a quiet, calmer place to relax. Here, too, the aviation theme is played out in the memorabilia on the walls. Banquettes line the dance floor which, when not in

use for disco-ing, has tables and chairs set out on it. There is a D-J booth to provide the music and a small stage can accommodate live performances. The big band mural, by Kenneth Gore for Grand Illusions, provides the background for this lively entertainment venue In an area resembling an airport hangar, is the Game Room which is furnished with pool tables. Danine Alati, describing this project in Contract Design, said, "Going from the bar and lounge past the aviation mural into the game room, guests are aware of the very dissected zones of Rickenbaker which seeks to and seems to accomplish pleasing any and all guests."

The designer used inexpensive materials and in many cases salvaged furniture and banquettes that were reupholstered to create the exciting design of Rickenbakers. Faux finishes, splattered walls and concrete floors, open stud systems, colorful fabrics, plane models, parachutes, industrial finishes and the American flag add up to a fun and cozy place to hang out.

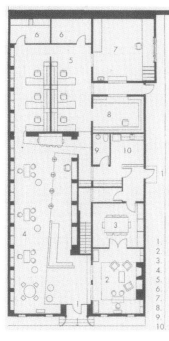

key

SPLIT ROCK BAR & GRILL

MINNEAPOLIS/ST. PAUL AIRPORT, MN

Design ▪ Sunderland Innerspace Design,
Vancouver, Canada
Photography ▪ Sarri & Forrai Photography,
Minneapolis, MN

Designed for "the traveler in transition," Split Rock Bar & Grill is located on a busy concourse in the Minneapolis/St. Paul Airport. The client's request was that the space "tell a story" that is indigenous to Minnesota: a story that takes the visitor through the backroads of the country.

The major theme and the motifs are all introduced out front on the facade which combines birch trees as dividers between the windows, the native stone laid in courses as a base, the rough hewn timber that frames the iron door and the raised metal signage over the door. Walking through the front door is like stepping into a forest of birch trees that grow in northern Minnesota. "The trees are visually appealing with their white bark offering a serene backdrop to a busy concourse." Some of the floor-to-ceiling trees support circular table tops that are surrounded by pull-up stools set out on the green slate floor. The stone faced bar is topped with a replica of the infamous Split Rock lighthouse that has served as a beacon against the harsh Northern Superior waters for over 50 years. The lighthouse is still a popular tourist attraction.

Throughout, the warm interior pays tribute to, and employs the geographical elements of, the state. "The use and variety of materials and finishes work in unison to create an outdoor experience indoors." Pipestone, a native stone inherent in the area, is used in many ways: applied to walls, to face the bar, and surround the fireplace. Another valuable asset of Minnesota is the iron ore that has been mined here for a long time. Sunderland uses iron on the entrance doors, for the hand forged wall sconces, the ceiling light feature and to outline the serpentine banquette that serves to separate the bar from the café.

From the sweeping seating area, travelers-in-waiting can enjoy a warm fire when the weather turns—and it does turn in Minneapolis. One side of the restaurant is a "wheat wall and silo booth" that represents the crossroads between the forest, the farming and the mining. Minnesota is a "gateway to the American Plains."

Overall, the "story" is wordlessly told again and again to each visitor that travels through the door of the Split Rock Bar & Grill.

BEIGNET'S CAFÉ

SEASIDE HEIGHTS, NJ

Design ▪ JBD/JGA: Judd Brown Design & Jefferson Design Group, Warwick, RI

Photography ▪ Warren Jagger

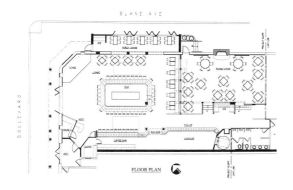

Located in Seaside Heights, NJ is Beignet's Café which was designed by Judd Brown Design & Jefferson Group Architects of Warwick, RI. The design concept was to "capture the essence and energy of a New Orleans street front bar and grill" while still maintaining a sophisticated level of design. Some of the design challenges included creating a curbside appeal that was somewhat upscale on a seasonally busy seaside street and overcoming the limitations set by the concrete block construction, small windows and open framing.

The café now features an open bar and kitchen area with a large exhibition cooking line. Together with the Raw Bar, there is an opportunity for the chef and crew line to "play a leading role in the restaurant theater." The murals, by Gene Mollica Studios, create the New Orleans feeling with their depictions of street life. Each mural is

framed by tall, louvered shutters and by "looking out of the windows" the entire space opens up. The specially designed and installed mosaic tile floors add to "the appearance of greater depth" to the space while visually directing the diner's eye towards the focal kitchen. Signature light fixtures are used to identify the areas of the café: the seating area, the bar and the rest rooms. The overhead yellow illuminated signs also signal the different areas in the 110-seat establishment.

The success of this project has not only led to more commissions for the designers from this client but it has had a great effect on the revitalization of the seaside location. New capital is being invested in further development on the street and Beignet's Café is being used as an example for future architectural expectations in federal grant applications.

DICK CLARK'S A B DINER

SCHAUMBURG, IL

Design ▪ AAD, Scottsdale, AZ
Principals ▪ Michael Stevenson, AIA & Carl Schaffer, AIA
Studio Directors ▪ Doug Tener/William Weikart
Development Team ▪ Ron Laird/Daryl Reynolds
For Dick Clark Restaurants ▪ Art Carlson &
Jack Woodward
Photography ▪ Anthony May Photography, Chicago

Recently opened on The Street at Woodfield, an entertainment and retail complex in Schaumburg, IL, is the new concept café that combines American Diner cuisine with Rock 'N' Roll nostalgia. Dick Clark's AB Diner takes us back in time to something as new as tomorrow. The diner-style format has been tailored for "high entertainment environments" like this location which is next to a 20-screen movie house. Designed by AAD of Scottsdale, AZ in conjunction with Art Carlson and Jack Woodward of Dick Clark Restaurants, it recalls the era of the American Bandstand TV Show hosted by Dick Clark. "We wanted to create the nostalgic, inviting atmosphere of the classic American diner. We also used the American Bandstand motif to celebrate more than 30 years of Rock 'N' Roll music," said William Weikart of AAD.

Guests follow the "dance steps" on the sidewalk into the 5000 sq. ft. space. Inside, overhead there are a series of sound domes that play music from specific eras as guests move beneath them. Graphic images of records and CDs of the specific periods are embedded in the floors under the domes. A highlight of the Diner is the soda fountain counter which was designed with an eclectic mix of motifs and materials such as glass blocks backlit with neon lighting, vintage looking, quilted, stainless steel banding, and black and white tile floors. Inside the

dining room it is red naugahyde seats and reproductions of juke boxes that recall the old fashioned diners. A giant mural, 44 ft. long by eight ft. high, is designed as a time-line and it features a collage of actual photos of American Bandstand shows. Carrying through the theme are the theatrical stage lights that help to immortalize the American Bandstand set.

This is a fun and "in" place to go for American Diner cuisine such as burgers, malts, shakes, fries—and other "comfort" foods.

BEN'S KOSHER DELI

WOODBURY, NY

Design ▪ Judd Brown Design & Jefferson Group Architects, Warwick, RI
Photography ▪ Warren Jagger

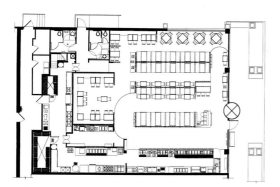

A New York Deli is as special and unique a dining experience as is a visit to a bistro in Paris, a caffe in Rome or a diner somewhere on Rte 66 in Arizona. It is a piece of Americana and Ben's Kosher Deli was designed by JBD/JGA of Warwick, RI as a kind of fun and spirited setting for a very special kind of gastronomic adventure. The challenge was to create a casual and relaxed setting which would not only appeal to the ex-New Yorkers who now live in this suburb of NYC but would also appeal to others, in other parts of the country, when Ben's rolls out across the nation as a chain of NY Deli operations.

Working within a limited footprint, the designers had to accommodate a long deli line, a take-out sales area, a support kitchen, storage areas, a private party room and, of course, compartmentalized seating for over 110 eat-in guests. In addition there were the high, industrial ceilings to contend with in the strip mall location. The designers used familiar NY icons to affect the atmosphere. The shape of the deli line was a natural for creating the feeling of train tracks winding through various NY neighborhoods. These neighborhoods were presented in bright, colorful and amusing murals on the fascia over the serving line. In keeping with the subway concept, there are turn-of-the-century subway "girders" and "arches" lazer cut from foam "to provide a low cost, visually effective design component." They stretch across the dine-in seating and also serve to divide without hiding the dining areas from the service areas. A map on the floor correlates sections of the restaurant with sections of NY such as Broadway, Times Square and Wall Street. It is reinforced with "visual prompts" such as graffiti art and arches to "create a symbolic rather than literal interpretation of the city."

Many of the interior walls are painted a soft, wheat-yellow color that brightens up the space without detracting from the delicious, colorful murals and the signage. Mosaic

floor tiles in a variety of combinations and patterns cover the floor and the Empire State Building and art deco are acknowledged in the stepped chair backs that complement the upholstered booths and banquettes. Lighting reinforces the subterranean station atmosphere with theatrical track spots, indirect lighting and fiber optic chandeliers.

To highlight the entrance and bring the restaurant into prominence, a bold marquee was applied to the facade. It creates "a beacon to welcome and extend hospitality to potential patrons, thereby overcoming the exterior sign limitations imposed by the lease with the strip mall." The marquee was inspired by the Statue of Liberty and the dazzling neon "crown" over the revolving doors along with the wide open, almost all-glass facade is most effective especially at night.

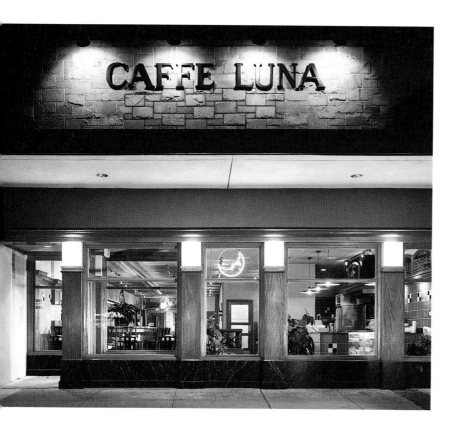

CAFFE LUNA

~~~~~~

NEWTON, MA

Design ▪ Morris Nathanson Design, Pawtucket, RI
Project Team ▪ Blase Gallo/Peter Niemitz/
Morris Nathanson
Production ▪ Neil Pereskula
Project Development ▪ Marve H. Cooper
Photography ▪ Warren Jagger

Caffe Luna brings the romance and charm of a northern Italian sidewalk café to the town of Newton, MA. As designed by Morris Nathanson Design, of Pawtucket, "the imagery derives its influences from the name—Caffe Luna: sky, night, moon and stars. We chose the planetary spheres, the faux painted star-lit sky to create the romance of Italian nights at outdoor cafes."

The café's owner, Jack Benjamin, was quite specific in how he wanted the space to be organized and function. The beer/wine and champagne bar was to be "typically European" and to appear up front and be very visible. "It was to act as a congenial meeting place, reception and holding area." The rotisserie was to be on exhibit but the kitchen was to be viewed selectively: the activity should be apparent but not necessarily the prep work. The take-out counter had to be accessible from the front but not interfere with the sit-down service. To accomplish this—plus two shopfronts—the designers were limited to a budget of $250,000.

In order to create the Italian ambiance "historical references were playfully used in a contemporary expression." The designers specified earthy colors, stucco finishes and terra cotta and black and white tiles like those used in the Duomo in Siena, The murals were to be "alla Firenze." The faux marble walls and the painted sky add to the overall look of the

space. To create a sense of "casual elegance" there are mullions designed as architectural pilasters, mahogany with accents of teal and maroon, gilt moldings, and iron railings that further enhance the feeling of an outdoor piazza. Pedestals with interior light columns establish an "architectural rhythm of space" while they suggest the ruins of ancient Rome and astrology—the science born in Italy.

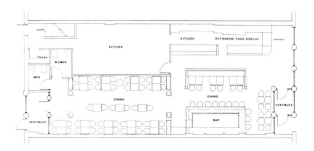

NORDSTROM'S CAFÉ

PERIMETER MALL, ATLANTA, GA

Design ▪ Engstrom Design Group, San Rafael, CA

Design Team ▪ Jennifer Johnson, AIA/Jeff Ellis, AIA/Nancy Kalter, AIA and Wenli Lin

Consulting Interior Designer ▪ Barbara Hofling

Architect ▪ Hayashida Architects

Photography ▪ Rion Rizzo/Creative Sources, Atlanta, GA

The new prototype for Nordstrom's Café was designed by the Engstrom Design Group of San Rafael, CA. Already realized in two locations, the Atlanta project is shown here, the results are already in and soon 15 additional cafes will be in working order. The new café has been created as a high quality food service in the Nordstrom department store to satisfy the Nordstrom patron.

The design and food presentation concept is based on a European marketplace. Patrons may pass through a "lively quick service" line which features artfully prepared and presented gourmet sandwiches, freshly tossed salads, pizzas, paninis, and pastas—served at appointed stations. Some future cafes, like the Overland Park one, will integrate a full service option as well.

To create the desired "old world" ambiance and also reiterate Nordstrom's fashion and quality position, Engstrom Design Group added many rich materials and details. There is the scalloped, solid cherry millwork, painted pressed tin ceilings and woodwork and large porcelain pavers as a "complementary architectural backdrop in

which the color and texture of food take center stage." The same care to detail extends to the display areas where the cherry wood shelves, dividers and fixtures all testify to the quality of Nordstrom's retail food products. The food presentation is enhanced by the use of the low voltage spots.

"Contemporary design elements update the European marketplace thematic while establishing continuity with the modern retail environment outside." The elegant soffits and ceiling coffers highlight and delineate the different areas in the restaurant and juxtaposed with the "old world" details are contemporary furnishings, fabrics and lighting. Contributing to the success of the café design is the mix of seating options which adds to the comfort level and the degree of sophistication of the dining experience.

Decorative signage accentuates each food station and it serves to direct the diner and also allows them to quickly by-pass stations that do not concern them. Consistent with the European marketplace theme, the signage borrows images from paintings of food done in the Renaissance period. The images are framed in forged iron, art nouveau inspired metalwork.

The Café will become a featured addition in all future, to-be-built, Nordstrom Department stores.

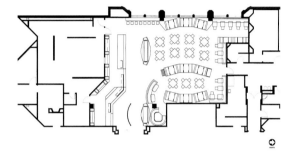

S A L U T E !

~~~~~~

N E W   Y O R K ,   N Y

Design ▪ Tree House Design Ltd., New York
Principal ▪ Julius "Jack" Baum
Photography ▪ Peter Paige Associates,
Harrington Park, NJ

1. Coat Room
2. Hostess
3. Bar
4. Cafe
5. Raised Dining
6. Dining Area
7. Pick-Up Counter
8. Display Kitchen
9. Pizza Oven
10. Take-Out Counter
11. Restrooms
12. Kitchen

The challenge for Jack Baum of Tree House Design was to meld a traditionally inspired rural Italian atmosphere into an urbane, 6000 sq. ft. café. The former drugstore space, located in a 25 story office building on Madison Ave. did not lend itself easily to a successful restaurant layout. It was a long and narrow space, on a corner site, and it had a few windows, but they faced 39th St.

The designer's solution was to place an island bar/café near the Madison Ave. entrance and thus use the corner space for high visibility from the street. "By opening the storefront to the bar only with operable, finished wood doors, it added the requisite excitement along both facades with the perception of the bar as a separate entity."

The bar/café appears to be separated from the main dining room by a simple, full height, wood and glass screen. This also makes it possible to permit smoking in the bar/café since it has its own powerful ventilation system. To break up the long run of the dining room, the open kitchen was set at the far, opposite end of the space and a platform was erected on the interior side of the center columns. This "stepping down" affords all the diners "a sense of action from each direction within the restaurant and emphasizes the centric nature of the dining room." Due to the limited budget, few resources were left for front-of-the-house design after the installation of the kitchen and the mechanical systems. The designer used inexpensive decorative devices to "increase the sense of style and budget."

There is striped faux painting on the columns along with the use of wood and stone multiple finishes on the floor

which also mirrors the pattern of the ceiling. The beams on the ceiling are recalled through the use of negative space: they rise up into the ceiling rather than extend down towards the floor. The concealed lighting, in the beams, accentuates "the tailored urban atmosphere."

The open kitchen is decorated with a wood burning oven that is highlighted with hand-painted, glazed tiles. Similar tiles add vibrant color to the food pick-up counter that runs the length of the open kitchen. Together they create a brilliant and color filled proscenium for the gastronomic stage. A take-out counter backs up to the kitchen. The retail area also is trimmed with the painted tiles plus quarter sawn mahogany, granite and polished brass.

THE HOUSE CAFÉ

HAMPSTEAD, LONDON, U.K.

Design ▪ Four IV Design Consultants, London
Photography ▪ Andrew Peppard

Adding to the "cool cafes" and the "hot" retail food outlets in Rosslyn Hill in Hampstead, a northern London neighborhood, is the House Café designed by Four IV Design Consultants.

To introduce the modernity and up-to-the-minute essence of The House, the design firm created a nine dot, "H" logo and then carried that graphic symbol into the retail establishment. The simple facade consists of two full length, all-glass windows flanking the central glass door which is framed in copper. Copper is also used to outline the glazed areas. The illuminated, blade sign shows off the "H" in the nine dot arrangement in blue on white. Red/orange lettering on frosted disks, applied to the front windows, highlights the offerings within.

"The interiors approach we have taken is one that is clean, innovative and modern, in line with the fresh, honest premium ingredients on the menu whilst ensuring a comfortable and enjoyable atmosphere," said Chris Dewar-Dixon, creative director at Four IV. The creamy beige and light wood walls and natural timber floors are accented by the bright signature blue color that surfaces the food service bar and the display cases. The long, narrow space is further accentuated by the long, wood topped counter that stretches along one of the long walls and the square stools and round tables that follow the same line. Overhead there are two light troughs. One is filled with focusable spots that illuminate the table tops while the other contains decorative red/orange disks. Wall washers, hidden behind this light trough, lights up the service areas, bars, and merchandise display shelves along the shop wall. To somewhat open the space, Four IV has played with mirrors. There are large, reflective mirrors placed along the wood sheathed wall and that tends to break up the shop into three segments. Stretched across the rear wall is a mirror that has the "H" logo etched on it. The logo also appears on the packaging, the coffee cups, bags and the boxes filled with the brand name chocolates.

Throughout, the designers have balanced the demands of sit-in comfort with the take-out customer flow. Most of the take-out is located up-front near the door while the sit-ins are towards the rear of the space.

TOON LAGOON COMIC STRIP CAFÉ

ORLANDO, FL

Design ▪ Fitch, Worthington, OH
Principal in charge ▪ Mark Artu
Project Manager ▪ Jon Baines
Design Director, Retail ▪ Christian Davies
Design Director, Restaurants ▪ Bruce Shepherd
Sr. Retail Designer ▪ Caryn Keller & Lynn Rosenbaum
Sr. Graphic Designer ▪ Paul Lycett
Implementation Architect ▪ Randy Miller/Steve Pottschmidt/Joe Klamert
Graphic Designer ▪ Terri Lubomski

CLIENT'S DESIGN TEAM
Project Architect ▪ Richard Krent, UIOA Retail Team
Interiors Manager ▪ Renee Samels, UIOA Retail Team
Theme Production Manager ▪ Audri Beck, UIOA Retail Team

Photography ▪ Mark Steele, Columbus, OH

Set up as the main eatery on Toon Lagoon Island in Universal Studios' new theme park in Orlando, FL is The Comic Strip Café. It was designed to service from 600–2000 guests in an hour. It was designed by Fitch of Worthington, OH, working with a Universal Studios design team as an international food court that serves five types of fast food cuisine.

Drawing inspiration from the classic Sunday funnies, the designers created a fun experience where people are moved through quickly and efficiently without ever feeling pressured, harried or rushed. The designers at Fitch worked with the basic floor plan and queuing patterns organized by Universal Studios. "Our contribution was to increase the efficiency of the ordering and dining experience while still creating an environment that embodies and brings to life the 2-D comic strip theme." Graphics was the solution.

Information conveyance was crucial. Graphics had to keep the people moving, provide them with information, and keep the overall feeling fun and lively. "It is all information

about menu choices, where to go next, etc." There are no comic characters in the queue graphics. Rather it is done with "expression bubbles"—the talk balloons that float over the heads of the comic strip characters. There are no distractions: keep the people informed of the options and keep them moving along. Once the guest has his food and is seated the character-oriented graphics appear. "Then characters and theming become important again, once again surrounding guests with the experience of theme through large scale reproductions of strips and characters." These panels also help to screen off the seated diners from the diners-to-be still on the line.

JOSE QUERVO TEQUILERIA

PHOENIX, AZ

Design ▪ AAD, Scottsdale, AZ
Principal in charge ▪ Carl F. Schaffer, AIA
Studio Director ▪ Keith Sullivan
Design Director ▪ Jennifer Reynolds
Development Team ▪ Tom Higgins/Rodney Jakes/Stacy Molnar/Sudeep Dey

CLIENT'S DESIGN TEAM
Dir. of Design & Construction ▪ Perry Brush
Development & General Manager ▪ Terry Ell
Photography ▪ Norton Photography, Phoenix

Like the Arizona Roadhouse, also designed by AAD of Scottsdale, AZ, Jose Quervo Tequileria is located in the Phoenix Sky Harbor International Airport. It is a 2800 sq. ft. space that is divided into two areas: the "traditional" and the "fun."

The Jose Quervo Tequila brand name appears on the facade along with the new "Tequileria" logo. The "boogie man" icon was especially designed and incorporated into the new symbol. A mosaic lizard, crafted from bits of broken ceramic tiles is illuminated with a halo of light while, underfoot, a glass mosaic tile rosette (a Quervo trademark) has been laid in the entry.

The visitor enters into the "fun" area. Here the floor is part cobblestone and part saltillo tile. The custom table tops are decorated with sayings and icons of the Quervo brand. The chairs have zigzag backs and they are multicolored-adding to the high spirits of the space. Focal in this section is the bar with its resin covered top embedded with Quervo brand labels. The front of the bar is stained corrugated metal. Over the bar hang Mexican tin star-lights and "Release Your Inner Lizard" (the Quervo motto) is pin mounted on the soffit. An amusing and educational promotional film about Jose Quervo Tequila is played and replayed on the video screens.. There are two, multi-colored, lizard shaped counters. A rebar and wood railing separates the bar and the stand-up area from the general

seating area. The wall at the end of the bar houses "La Cucina": a pass-through window which connects the Tequileria with the Blue Burrito Grill.

The dining room is more "traditional" and it is divided into three bays that reflect the tradition and history of the Tequila brand. The space is furnished with faux chiseled stone tables and "equipales" which are chairs with woven wooden seats and rounded, waxed leather backs. The leather gains in character as it ages. The floor is paved with baked tiles set within a criss-cross of ceramic wood planks. The ceiling is traditional: latilla and viga. It is constructed of the actual skeletons of the saguaro cactus and wooden cross beams. The walls are faux painted and glazed finished and the hand painted murals complete the environment along with authentic Mexican artifacts and crafts.

L O O N G B A R

S A N   F R A N C I S C O ,   C A

Design ▪ Studio Architectura/MBH Architects,
Alameda, CA

Photography ▪ Doug Salin

Loongbar—the Chinese word for dragon—was designed by Studio Architectura & MBH Architects of Alameda, CA for Chef Mark Miller. Located in a gutted, 11,000 sq. ft. space that was a movie house built in 1908, the design "brings together Asian design elements with contemporary concepts of space and comfort."

Diners enter at the dramatically lit mezzanine and pass through an arched, celadon tinted "Moon Gate." From there they descend down the sweeping, two story staircase to reach the dining room. Before passing through the Moon Gate, to the right, is a dimly illuminated, intimate bar/lounge with a marvelous view of the San Francisco Bay. The bar has a metallic red and black bar and Chinese glass tables nestle around the grand piano. The light is diffused through a shoji screen that is suspended overhead and 40 guests can be seated here.

Stephen Samuelson, the principal architect, said, "We needed to bring the large volume of space down to a personal level." His solution was to divide the overall space into a series of distinct spaces with a natural flow from one to the other. The flow now goes from the mezzanine bar and private dining room down the stairs into the main dining room. The glass walled dining room, on the mezzanine, overlooks the main floor and remains "aloof and apart." The space is "serene yet dramatic with arches, porthole windows and theatrical lighting"—all contained in the old brick structure. The main dining room which can accommodate 150 diners is a mix of round tables, booths, banquettes and a corner table surrounded by diaphanous curtains. The interior is plush with velvet chairs, a palette of dark reds, yellows, and greens "melded in Zen-like fashion." The shades of cinnabar, ocher and celadon sum-

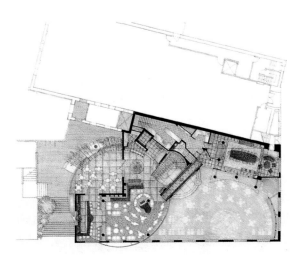

mon up images of the Orient while layers of gold leaf add luminescence to the colors. "Rich colors, symbolic motifs and a subtle play of light and shadow create a setting filled with mystery, romance and surprise."

A focal point in the dining room is the 12-ft. food altar. Throughout the restaurant the dragon in the name is represented by the wrapped columns and the "scales" etched into the concrete. Even the sinuous curves of the banquettes are designed to suggest the slithering of the dragon.

Loongbar is located in the Powerhouse Building in a popular tourist destination, The art of Feng Shui was implemented into the design. "We wanted the restaurant to fit into its natural landscape nestled between the San Francisco Bay and a sloping hillside—both omens of prosperity." Asian temples also served as a source of inspiration where attention is drawn inward rather than outward.

The grand, supercolossal, 40,000 sq. ft. new WB Stage 16 restaurant is located in the equally sensational Venetian Hotel/Casinos in Las Vegas. Fitch of Worthington, OH. working with the Warner Bros. Design staffs recreated "the glamourous behind-the-scenic allure of four Warner Bros. movie sets" which now serve up to 300 guests in an upscale atmosphere. The name is actually a tribute to Stage 16 on the Warner Bros. Studio lot in Burbank. It is the largest and most famous of all the sound stages.

WB STAGE 16

LAS VEGAS, NV

Design ▪ Fitch, Worthington, OH
Principal in charge ▪ Mark Artus
Project Manager ▪ Lynn Rosenblum
Sr. Environmental Designer ▪ Todd Rowland
Environmental Designer ▪ Michele Hofer
Communications Designer ▪ Brandy Shearer
Sr. Implementation Designer ▪ Steve Pottschmidt
Implementation Designer ▪ Allison Tuller
Architectural Designer ▪ Tim Baker
AAD Design ▪ Timothy Pleger, Architect
Client Design Team ▪ WB Stage 16, Orlando, FL
President ▪ Gerard O'Riordan
VP Development ▪ Mark McClenney
VP Operations ▪ John Baydale
VP Merchandising ▪ Patrick Hartnett, Warner Bros., Burbank, CA
Supervisor ▪ Ed Strang, WB Studios Scenic Art Dept.
Photography ▪ Mark Steele, Columbus, OH

The diner has the choice of four different movie experiences. There is Rick's Café American made famous in the movie "Casablanca," the lounge set that served Frank Sinatra and the Rat Pack in "Oceans 11," the rooftop terrace that overlooks "Batman's Gotham City" skyline and the art deco inspired "We're in the Money" set from the "Golddiggers of 1933." The designers studied the actual construction drawings of the sets used in the four films and checked with historical documentation, the WB archives and actual film footage "to ensure authentic reproductions." To give these spaces an added element of reality, the exact seating plans and table locations from Rick's Café and the Tropicana Hotel were followed. Background sound effects and music from the actual films were integrated into the ambiance of the space "to evoke the original movie environment."

Lynn Rosenblum, Fitch's associate VP and creative director of the project said, "With the design of these spaces, we've tried to deliver the unmistakable appeal of the backstage world of Hollywood movie making. We've left no detail out of the development of these full scale recreations of some of the most vivid, elegant and dramatic stage sets from Warner Bros.' history."

To reinforce the feeling that these are "stage sets," Fitch worked with visible sound stage elements such as exposed beams, wood scaffold structures, green bed track lights, and tromp l'oeil painted scrim backgrounds. For the "Oceans 11" set, the designers recreated Jack's Velvet Lounge, an upstairs bar area that overlooks the Las Vegas strip. They included a backstage area that has been "dressed" as if for an impromptu cast party. In this way the designers have effectively continued the studio lot narrative that runs through the whole restaurant.

Several non-dining areas are included in WB Stage 16. The Music Bar is a casual video bar that features music by WB entertainers. The Prop Department serves as a retail shop for licensed brand WB merchandise in a setting that resembles a movie lot properties department. A full size auditorium is also available for conferences or film screenings—Warner Bros. films, of course.

CAFÉ SBARRO

GARDEN CITY, NY

Design ▪ Tree House Design ,LTD.
Julius "Jack" Baum
Photography ▪ Stephan Carr Photography, NY

According to Julius S. "Jack" Baum, principal of Tree House Design, Ltd. and designer of the new Café Sbarro in the Roosevelt Field Mall in Garden City, NY , this design "is a successful attempt to meld traditional Café style and atmosphere with the modern expectations of fast quick service desirable in a shopping mall." The challenge for the designer was to transform the former 2500 sq. ft. bank space into a more upscale version of what diners have come to expect from Sbarro—a highly successful, self-service food operation.

To emphasize the Café environment, the design calls for a bright and open dining room. Large porcelain tiles of several color variations are used to cover the floor while also delineating areas of function. To further the image of an upscale Café, the designer selected a mahogany finished wainscot with Venetian plaster walls above which are rich gold in color and scored in white. Since wine is an integral part of café dining, there is a handsome mahogany wine display cabinet set along one wall.

The loose table seating consists of tables topped with verde marble bullnose edged in mahogany. The chairs are a modern interpretation of the classic Café chair and they have open slat backs and are finished with wood contoured seats. Some of the walls are lined with upholstered banquettes. The service bar reiterates the verde marble and mahogany in its design. Giant pizza ovens, under stainless steel canopies, cover most of the wall behind the service line.

Throughout there is colorful artwork. There is a mural in the cove around the perimeter of the space "which reflects traditional Italian designs taken from real, hand-painted ceramic dishes." The actual dishes that served as the inspiration for the artwork are displayed on the walls in a corner of the Café. A single, light colored wall is dominated by a checkerboard design that alternates squares of painted motifs with squares of mahogany.

Café Sbarro has proven to be a great success with diners in this upscaled mall.

LA CUCINA

WEST HARTFORD, CT

Design ▪ Tree House Design, Ltd., New York, NY
Julius S. "Jack" Baum
Photography ▪ Stephan J. Carr Photography

Though La Cucina, situated in the West Farms Mall in West Hartford, CT has limited waiter and china service, it still comes across as a beautiful and successful blend of traditional café styling and modern, quick service. "The café tries to meet the expectations of busy shoppers with an atmosphere of a more traditional, full-service café."

To complement the "traditional Italian country" menu, Julius S. "Jack" Baum of Tree House Design, Ltd. introduced warm Venetian plaster finishes on the walls and rustic ceramic tiles on the floor. These are complemented by the abundance of finished mahogany used on the wainscoting and on one entire accent wall. Small illuminated niches pierce that wall and topiary plant arrangements are set into the openings. The tables are topped with rosa marble framed with a bullnose edge of mahogany. Traditional trattoria-style chairs are used with the tables.

Visible behind an etched glass window is the open kitchen. The traditional pizza oven is set into an arched opening behind the food display line. The dark red and white tiles that frame the Italian glazed, white ceramic tile faced oven highlight the area. The deep mahogany colored wood that is used to face the service counter is topped with rosa granite. Above the counter is a framework of wrought iron which supports track lights and custom, frosted glass pendants. The lighting throughout is generally indirect with dramatic frosted glass uprights on the columns providing much of it. The illusion of widening the narrow space is accomplished by the use of a large scale mural of the Italian countryside on the wall. It is rendered in yellows, golds, greens and faded blues by the Vermont artist Alex Baker. It does create the feeling of spaciousness as well as a "view of the out-of-doors."

Located within sight of water, Cosmic Boat—a dining/entertainment complex outside of Rome—was designed with a nautical theme. Studio Ciccotti was inspired by the seaside location, and the bowling alley fittings that respond to special lighting effects to create wave-like patterns. From these the name evolved. Throughout the dual level, multi-area space one is surrounded by waves, by bowed shapes, by undulating forms, and by "the canalization of the air conditioning system which leaves the pipes and ducts in clear view in the ceiling."

Shiny sheets of embossed and patterned aluminum and steel are bolted on to the bars that snake in and around. They are finished with black "waves" at the floor line. All the furniture is metal and is finished in gray/gray-blue colors. The seats are upholstered in festive marine colors like green, gold, orange and red. The booths in the restaurant area are upholstered in the same bright colors and they are combined with the shiny metal pull-up chairs that accompany the colorful laminate topped tables. Combined with dropped ceiling lights, the space recalls an American diner of the 1950s–1960s

In laying out the space the designers opted for an open look which would accommodate the bowling alleys, video game areas, billiard tables, internet rooms, two bars and the café. All important here is the central zone. This area

COSMIC BOAT

ROME, ITALY

Design ▪ Studio Ciccotti, Rome

serves many purposes. It holds the flow of entering guests; it separates the bar from the restaurant; and when needed it serves as the disco dance floor. On special nights referred to as "Cosmic Nights," the general lights are dimmed and the scanners, the strobe lights and the many color-filtered spots come together with the sound produced by the DJ (Disc Jockey) to create "a cosmic disco atmosphere." The DJ's console is set behind the bar.

An open atrium, in the center on this Central Zone, contains the embossed, metal-tread, staircase that leads to the lower level where the billiard tables are located. In the nautical tradition, the opening is surrounded by a metal pipe railing detailed with nautical wires pulled through that serve as a deterrent. The large, multi-colored couch recalls the "diner" style banquettes of the restaurant and picks up the same color palette. Deep marine blue upholstery appears on the bar stools in both bar areas. Overhead TV monitors continue the sense of fun, action and non-stop entertainment at Cosmic Boat.

ELROY'S

SAN FRANCISCO, CA

Design ▪ MBH Architects , Alameda CA.
Design Team ▪ Shawn Alexander / Clay Fry /
David Melling / Ken Lidiker
Photography ▪ Dennis Anderson Photography,
San Raphael, CA

Elroy's is more than a Café or a bar or a restaurant. It is an all consuming experience. The 15,000 sq. ft., 300 seat establishment is located at the corner of Beale & Folsom Sts. in San Francisco, in a retrofitted, six story historic building: The old Coffin-Reddington Building. Elroy's shares this building with luxury condominiums. Nicely fitted into the street level space is a restaurant, an open kitchen, a raised dining level, open terrace dining, three bars, an espresso bar and a "pool parlor" on the mezzanine. The southwest style cuisine is served in a tongue-in-cheek, eclectic setting.

The clients, Boulder Concepts, wanted an interior "that appears as if the Jetson's meet up with the Flintstone's." The architects/designers, MBH Architects, saw this as a fabulous opportunity to freely "create excitement with form and color." Upon entering Elroy's the guests are met by a two story high, cylindrical lava lamp. "Lighting has long been recognized as a critical design element in retail spaces and is fast becoming a signature piece of many higher end restaurants." For more effective lighting effects and opportunities, a projecting planar element extends out over the display kitchen from which custom lighting fixtures hang. They accentuate "the performance space." Directly opposite this feature and above the raised dining area along the exterior wall is a curved soffit. Between these two dominant architectural elements and featured throughout the space are dramatic custom light fixtures. Decorative motifs of the 1950s and 1960s-updated-appear and reappear.

The bar area is aglow with warm light from the textured glass that fills the space above and below the bar. On a mezzanine, there are four pool tables and a vista overlooking the main dining room. During the warmer months there are dining opportunities out on a covered deck. With its location "South of Market" Elroy's has become one of San Francisco's hottest dining spots.

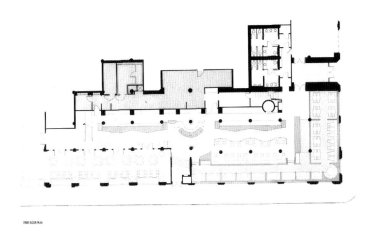

FIRST FLOOR PLAN

INDEX OF DESIGN FIRMS